PLANNING, PROGRAMMING, BUDGETING, AND EXECUTION
IN COMPARATIVE ORGANIZATIONS

VOLUME 1

Case Studies of China and Russia

MEGAN McKERNAN | STEPHANIE YOUNG | TIMOTHY R. HEATH
DARA MASSICOT | MARK STALCZYNSKI | IVANA KE
RAPHAEL S. COHEN | JOHN P. GODGES
HEIDI PETERS | LAUREN SKRABALA

Prepared for the Commission on Planning, Programming, Budgeting, and Execution Reform
Approved for public release; distribution is unlimited

RAND
CORPORATION

For more information on this publication, visit **www.rand.org/t/RRA2195-1**.

About RAND

The RAND Corporation is a research organization that develops solutions to public policy challenges to help make communities throughout the world safer and more secure, healthier and more prosperous. RAND is nonprofit, nonpartisan, and committed to the public interest. To learn more about RAND, visit www.rand.org.

Research Integrity

Our mission to help improve policy and decisionmaking through research and analysis is enabled through our core values of quality and objectivity and our unwavering commitment to the highest level of integrity and ethical behavior. To help ensure our research and analysis are rigorous, objective, and nonpartisan, we subject our research publications to a robust and exacting quality-assurance process; avoid both the appearance and reality of financial and other conflicts of interest through staff training, project screening, and a policy of mandatory disclosure; and pursue transparency in our research engagements through our commitment to the open publication of our research findings and recommendations, disclosure of the source of funding of published research, and policies to ensure intellectual independence. For more information, visit www.rand.org/about/principles.

RAND's publications do not necessarily reflect the opinions of its research clients and sponsors.

Published by the RAND Corporation, Santa Monica, Calif.
© 2024 RAND Corporation
RAND® is a registered trademark.

Library of Congress Cataloging-in-Publication Data is available for this publication.

ISBN: 978-1-9774-1252-2

Cover design by Peter Soriano; adimas/Adobe Stock images.

About This Report

The U.S. Department of Defense (DoD) Planning, Programming, Budgeting, and Execution (PPBE) process is a key enabler for DoD to fulfill its mission. But in light of a dynamic threat environment, increasingly capable adversaries, and rapid technological changes, there has been increasing concern that DoD's resource planning processes are too slow and inflexible to meet warfighter needs.[1] As a result, Congress mandated the formation of a legislative commission in Section 1004 of the National Defense Authorization Act for Fiscal Year 2022 to (1) examine the effectiveness of the PPBE process and adjacent DoD practices, particularly with respect to defense modernization; (2) consider potential alternatives to these processes and practices to maximize DoD's ability to respond in a timely manner to current and future threats; and (3) make legislative and policy recommendations to improve such processes and practices for the purposes of fielding the operational capabilities necessary to outpace near-peer competitors, providing data and analytical insight, and supporting an integrated budget that is aligned with strategic defense objectives.[2]

The Commission on PPBE Reform requested that the National Defense Research Institute provide an independent analysis of PPBE-like functions in selected other countries and other federal agencies. This report, part of a four-volume set, analyzes the defense budgeting processes of China and Russia. Volume 2 analyzes the defense budgeting processes of allied countries and partners. Volume 3 analyzes the PPBE-like processes of other U.S. federal agencies. Volume 4, an executive summary, distills key insights from these three analytical volumes. The commission will use insights from these analyses to derive potential lessons for DoD and recommendations to Congress on PPBE reform.

This report should be of interest to those concerned with the improvement of DoD's PPBE processes. The intended audience is mostly government officials responsible for such processes. The research reported here was completed in March 2023 and underwent security review with the sponsor and the Defense Office of Prepublication and Security Review before public release.

RAND National Security Research Division

This research was sponsored by the Commission on PPBE Reform and conducted within the Acquisition and Technology Policy Program of the RAND National Security Research Divi-

---

[1] See, for example, Section 809 Panel, *Report of the Advisory Panel on Streamlining and Codifying Acquisition Regulations*, Vol. 2 of 3, June 2018, pp. 12–13; Brendan W. McGarry, *DOD Planning, Programming, Budgeting, and Execution: Overview and Selected Issues for Congress*, Congressional Research Service, R47178, July 11, 2022, p. 1; and William Greenwalt and Dan Patt, *Competing in Time: Ensuring Capability Advantage and Mission Success Through Adaptable Resource Allocation*, Hudson Institute, February 2021, pp. 9–10.

[2] Public Law 117–81, National Defense Authorization Act for Fiscal Year 2022, December 27, 2021.

sion (NSRD), which operates the National Defense Research Institute (NDRI), a federally funded research and development center sponsored by the Office of the Secretary of Defense, the Joint Staff, the Unified Combatant Commands, the Navy, the Marine Corps, the defense agencies, and the defense intelligence enterprise.

For more information on the RAND Acquisition and Technology Policy Program, see www.rand.org/nsrd/atp or contact the director (contact information is provided on the webpage).

Acknowledgments

The authors thank the members of the Commission on PPBE Reform—Robert Hale, Ellen Lord, Jonathan Burks, Susan Davis, Lisa Disbrow, Eric Fanning, Peter Levine, Jamie Morin, David Norquist, Diem Salmon, Jennifer Santos, Arun Seraphin, Raj Shah, and John Whitley—and staff for their dedication and deep expertise in shaping this work. We extend special gratitude to the commission chair, the Honorable Robert Hale; the vice chair, the Honorable Ellen Lord; executive director Lara Sayer; and director of research Elizabeth Bieri for their guidance and support throughout this analysis. We would also like to thank the subject-matter experts on China and Russia who provided us with valuable insight on these countries' PPBE-like processes.

From NSRD, we thank Barry Pavel, vice president and director, and Mike Spirtas, associate director, along with then–acting director Christopher Mouton and associate director Yun Kang of NSRD's Acquisition and Technology Policy Program, for their counsel and tireless support. We also thank our RAND Corporation colleagues who provided input at various stages of this work, including Don Snyder, Michael Kennedy, Irv Blickstein, Brian Persons, Chad Ohlandt, Bonnie Triezenberg, Obaid Younossi, Clinton Reach, John Yurchak, Jeffrey Drezner, Brady Cillo, and Gregory Graff, as well as the team of peer reviewers who offered helpful feedback on individual case studies and cross-case study takeaways: Cynthia Cook, Colin Smith, Nathan Beauchamp-Mustafaga, and Jim Powers. Finally, we would like to thank Maria Falvo and Saci Haslam for their administrative assistance during this effort. The work is much improved by virtue of their inputs, but any errors remain the responsibility of the authors alone.

Dedication

These volumes are dedicated to Irv Blickstein, whose decades of experience in the U.S. Navy's PPBE community deeply informed this work and whose intellectual leadership as a RAND colleague for more than 20 years greatly enhanced the quality of our independent analysis for DoD's most-pressing acquisition challenges. Irv's kindness, motivation, and ever-present mentoring will be sorely missed.

Summary

Issue

The U.S. Department of Defense's (DoD's) Planning, Programming, Budgeting, and Execution (PPBE) System was originally developed in the 1960s as a structured approach for planning long-term resource development, assessing program cost-effectiveness, and aligning resources to strategies. Yet changes to the strategic environment, the industrial base, and the nature of military capabilities have raised the question of whether U.S. defense budgeting processes are still well aligned with national needs.

Congress, in its National Defense Authorization Act for Fiscal Year 2022, called for the establishment of a Commission on PPBE Reform, which took shape as a legislative commission in 2022.[3] As part of its data collection efforts, the Commission on PPBE Reform asked the National Defense Research Institute, a federally funded research and development center operated by the RAND National Security Research Division, to conduct case studies of budgeting processes across nine comparative organizations: five international defense organizations and four U.S. federal government agencies. The two international case studies of near-peer competitors China and Russia were specifically requested by Congress, while the other seven cases were selected in close partnership with the commission.

Approach

For all nine case studies, the research entailed extensive document reviews and structured discussions with subject-matter experts having experience in the budgeting processes of the selected international governments and other U.S. federal government agencies. Each case study was assigned a unique team with appropriate regional or organizational expertise. For the near-peer competitor cases, the assigned experts had the language skills and methodological training to facilitate working with primary sources in Chinese or Russian. The analysis was also supplemented by experts in the U.S. PPBE process, as applicable.

---

[3] Public Law 117–81, National Defense Authorization Act for Fiscal Year 2022, December 27, 2021.

Key Insights

The key insights from the case studies of China and Russia detailed in this volume are as follows:

- **China and Russia make top-down decisions about priorities and risks but face limitations in implementation.** Senior leaders in these countries have the authority to make top-down decisions, but realizing returns on those decisions is contingent on key social, economic, and other factors. In China, modernization efforts in such areas as jet engines and semiconductors have not yielded consistent outcomes; other determinative factors are long-term investment stability, innovation enablers, and a workforce with relevant expertise. In Russia, a significant increase in the defense budget for the war in Ukraine, along with the adoption of new mobilization laws, have run into limitations in industrial capacity, supply chain reliability, and the ability to call up required manpower, even through conscription.
- **China and Russia make long-term plans but have mechanisms for changing course in accordance with changing priorities.** Centralized decisionmaking in both countries can reduce the friction associated with course corrections, but China is less likely than Russia to face hard choices when it comes to reprioritizing because of China's economic growth over recent decades.
- **Especially in China, political leaders provide stable and sustained long-term support for military modernization priorities.** The lack of political opposition, the high degree of alignment between military and senior political leaders, and the sheer scale of military investment over several decades have facilitated the stable planning and long-term investments that are essential for making progress toward complex modernization priorities. In contrast, Russia has a ten-year armaments program supported by a three-year budget—a combination that, in theory, balances stability with flexibility. But, in reality, the three-year budget is aspirational and has been rapidly jettisoned without political or legal blowback, leaving defense industrial base companies in a vulnerable position over the long term.
- **China and Russia have weak mechanisms for avoiding graft or ensuring transparency, efficiency, effectiveness, and quality control in PPBE-like processes.** The power dynamics and the structures of decisionmaking in these countries provide limited guardrails for ensuring the efficiency, effectiveness, and oversight of investments. China's budgeting processes are hampered by clientelism (bribery), patronage (favoritism), and other forms of corruption that pervade the defense industries. China's authorities also regard their budget processes as lagging those of Western counterparts. Powerful state-owned enterprises continue to operate in a highly inefficient and wasteful manner, partly because of the political power they exert. Similarly, in Russia, defense spending is subject to corruption in the Ministry of Defense, cronyism throughout the defense industrial base, and a general lack of serious anticorruption measures.

- **Reforms in China and Russia have been designed to increase the oversight of resource allocation processes.** China, since at least the early 2000s, and Russia, since the 2020s, have recognized the inefficiencies and limited avenues for competing voices in their top-down budget processes. They have looked to other international models, including those used in the United States, for lessons on budget reforms. In accordance with centrally directed reforms, the People's Liberation Army has carried out multiple rounds of reforms in its budgeting and financial system. Chinese leaders have long recognized that the military's budget system, like that of the government overall, suffers from severe problems related to corruption and weak accountability. Russia's budget is based on best practices, such as the use of a three-year or medium-term expenditure framework, and prior to the invasion of Ukraine, fiscally conservative funding was allocated annually within reasonable constraints. Nonetheless, budget execution in Russia has few safeguards, little oversight, and meager quality control.

Although the 2022 National Defense Strategy calls out China and Russia as posing particular challenges to the United States and the international order, the nature of those challenges are distinct and situationally dependent. China and Russia have unique histories, economic conditions, industrial capacities, and military capabilities; thus, they pose separate challenges to the United States. Societal fundamentals for building military capability are critical factors in determining the success of military modernization; thus, it is unclear how much success can be meaningfully attributed to resource planning processes. Additional critical inputs to success include the following:

- workforce capacity, capabilities, and productivity
- the scale and focus of defense investment over time
- industrial capacity and capability
- industrial policy
- innovation policy.

China and Russia are also both extraordinarily different from the United States in terms of their political cultures, governance structures, and strategic orientations. Both have demonstrated that strong central authority can ensure that long-term planning (without opposition) aligns resources to priorities, and these countries are able to redirect resources to meet changing needs. However, there are constraints and trade-offs that come with a top-down approach. For example, it can hamper innovation and yield weak mechanisms for oversight and quality control of budget execution.

Given this context, the lessons for U.S. PPBE reform efforts cannot be directly applicable. In addition, there is immense information asymmetry: It is difficult to gain a complete picture of China's and Russia's budgetary processes from open-source reporting—in contrast to the abundance of open-source critiques of U.S. PPBE processes. The risk is that China's and Russia's processes may sound more ideal because of the lack of publicly available information about their execution. Despite these differences, the case studies suggest several considerations that are relevant for the United States.

The Commission on PPBE Reform is looking for potential lessons from the PPBE-like systems of competitor nations to improve DoD's PPBE System. The relevance of these lessons—particularly from China—will invariably be constrained by the differences in the U.S. political system.

DoD likely will not find a simple way of replicating China's advantages by imitation, given the stark differences between the governmental systems of the United States and China. However, finding analogous measures to achieve similar effects could be worthwhile. In particular, two types of measures could be beneficial for DoD budgeting practices: (1) finding ways to ensure sustained, consistent funding for priority projects over many years; and (2) delegating more authority and granting greater flexibility to project and program managers, without compromising accountability, so that they can make changes to stay in alignment with guidance as technologies and programs advance.

Russia can be fiscally conservative at the federal level, and its defense acquisition plans are often closely tied to military strategy and defense needs. However, opacity in multiple parts of Russia's PPBE-like process often perpetuates corruption and generates outputs of varying quality from the country's defense industry. Russia's system does not allow sufficient oversight to ensure that it works effectively or produces uniformly high-quality products.

Despite the frequent public discussion in the United States that oversight adds time to the DoD's PPBE processes, it is clear from the experiences of China and Russia that oversight is a critical element that ultimately helps in the successful deployment of capabilities for use during operations and, therefore, should not be haphazardly traded away for speed during resource allocation.

Contents

About This Report iii
Summary v
Figures and Tables xi

CHAPTER 1
Introduction 1
  Evolution of DoD's PPBE System 2
  Research Approach and Methods 6
  Near-Peer Competitors Focus 8
  Structure of This Report 13

CHAPTER 2
China 15
Timothy Heath and Ivana Ke
  Overview of China's Defense Budgeting Process 20
  Analysis of China's Defense Budgeting Process 29
  Lessons from China's Defense Budgeting Process 33
  Conclusion 35

CHAPTER 3
Russia 39
Dara Massicot and Mark Stalczynski
  Russia's Defense Industrial Base: A Primer 40
  Overview of Russia's Defense Budgeting Process 43
  Analysis of Russia's Defense Budgeting Process 61
  Lessons from Russia's Defense Budgeting Process 64

CHAPTER 4
Key Insights from China and Russia Case Studies 69
  Key Insights 69
  Applicability of These Insights to DoD's PPBE System 71
  Summary of the Governance and Budgetary Systems of Near-Peer Competitor Case
    Studies 73

Abbreviations 79
References 81

Figures and Tables

Figures

1.1. DoD's PPBE Process (as of September 2019) 4
1.2. Military Expenditures, by Country, 1993–2021 10
2.1. China's Official Defense Spending, 2007–2018 16
2.2. The Budgeting Process in China 21
2.3. China's Annual Military Budget Cycle 27
3.1. Annual Budget Process in Russia 44
3.2. Russia's Total Defense Spending and Share of GDP 46
3.3. State Defense Order as a Share of Russia's National Defense Budget 47

Tables

2.1. Key Actors in the PLA's Budgeting Process 23
2.2. Lessons from China's Defense Budgeting Process 35
3.1. Major Russian Defense Firms Controlled by Rostec 42
3.2. History of Russia's State Armaments Programs 48
3.3. Subchapters of National Defense in Russia's 2021 and 2023 Budgets 58
3.4. Lessons from Russia's Defense Budgeting Process 67
4.1. Governance: U.S. and Comparative Nation Government Structures and Key
      Participants 73
4.2. Governance: U.S. and Comparative Nation Spending Controls and Decision
      Supports 74
4.3. Planning: U.S. and Comparative Nation Inputs and Outputs 74
4.4. Planning: U.S. and Comparative Nation Strategic Emphasis and Stakeholders ... 75
4.5. Programming: U.S. and Comparative Nation Resource Allocations and
      Time Frames 75
4.6. Programming: U.S. and Comparative Nation Stakeholders 76
4.7. Budgeting: U.S. and Comparative Nation Time Frames and Major Categories 76
4.8. Budgeting: Selected U.S. and Comparative Nation Stakeholders 77
4.9. Execution: U.S. and Comparative Nation Budgetary Flexibilities and
      Reprogramming 77
4.10. Execution: U.S. and Comparative Nation Assessment 78

CHAPTER 1

Introduction

In light of a dynamic threat environment, increasingly capable adversaries, and rapid technological changes, there has been increasing concern that the U.S. Department of Defense's (DoD's) resource planning processes are too slow and inflexible to meet warfighter needs.[1] DoD's Planning, Programming, Budgeting, and Execution (PPBE) System was originally developed in the 1960s as a structured approach for planning long-term resource development, assessing program cost-effectiveness, and aligning resources to strategies. Yet changes to the strategic environment, the industrial base, and the nature of military capabilities have raised the question of whether DoD's budgeting processes are still well aligned with national security needs.

To consider the effectiveness of current resource planning processes for meeting national security needs and to explore potential policy options to strengthen those processes, Congress called for the establishment of a commission on PPBE reform in Section 1004 of the National Defense Authorization Act for Fiscal Year 2022.[2] The Commission on PPBE Reform took shape as a legislative commission in 2022, consisting of 14 appointed commissioners, each drawing on deep and varied professional expertise in DoD, Congress, and the private sector. In support of the work, the commission collected data, conducted analyses, and developed a broad array of inputs from external organizations, including federally funded research and development centers, to develop targeted insights of particular interest to the commission. The commission asked the RAND National Defense Research Institute to contribute to this work by conducting case studies of nine comparative organizations: five international defense organizations and four other U.S. federal government agencies. Two of the interna-

---

[1] See, for example, Section 809 Panel, *Report of the Advisory Panel on Streamlining and Codifying Acquisition Regulations*, Vol. 2 of 3, June 2018, pp. 12–13; Brendan W. McGarry, *DOD Planning, Programming, Budgeting, and Execution: Overview and Selected Issues for Congress*, Congressional Research Service, R47178, July 11, 2022, p. 1; and William Greenwalt and Dan Patt, *Competing in Time: Ensuring Capability Advantage and Mission Success Through Adaptable Resource Allocation*, Hudson Institute, February 2021, pp. 9–10.

[2] Public Law 117–81, National Defense Authorization Act for Fiscal Year 2022, December 27, 2021, Section 1004(f)(1) reads as follows:

> Compare the planning, programming, budgeting, and execution process of the Department of Defense, including the development and production of documents including the Defense Planning Guidance, . . . the Program Objective Memorandum, and the Budget Estimate Submission, with similar processes of private industry, other Federal agencies, and other countries.

tional case studies—of near-peer competitors China and Russia—were specifically called for by Congress, and additional cases were selected in close partnership with the commission.[3]

This report is Volume 1 in a four-volume set, three of which present case studies conducted in support of the Commission on PPBE Reform. The accompanying volumes focus on selected U.S. partners and allies (*Planning, Programming, Budgeting, and Execution in Comparative Organizations: Vol. 2, Case Studies of Selected Allied and Partner Nations*) and selected non-DoD federal government agencies (*Planning, Programming, Budgeting, and Execution in Comparative Organizations: Vol. 3, Case Studies of Selected Non-DoD Federal Agencies*).[4] Volume 4, an executive summary, distills key insights from these three analytical volumes.[5]

Evolution of DoD's PPBE System

The Planning, Programming, and Budgeting System (PPBS), the precursor to DoD's PPBE process, took shape in the first decades after World War II and was introduced into DoD in 1961 by then–Secretary of Defense Robert McNamara.[6] Drawing on new social science methods, such as program budgeting and systems analysis, the PPBS was designed to provide a structured approach to weigh the cost-effectiveness of potential defense investments. A central assertion of PPBS's developers was that strategy and costs needed to be considered

---

[3] Pub. L. 117-81, Section 1004(f) requires "a review of budgeting methodologies and strategies of near-peer competitors to understand if and how such competitors can address current and future threats more or less successfully than the United States."

[4] Megan McKernan, Stephanie Young, Andrew Dowse, James Black, Devon Hill, Benjamin J. Sacks, Austin Wyatt, Nicolas Jouan, Yuliya Shokh, Jade Yeung, Raphael S. Cohen, John P. Godges, Heidi Peters, and Lauren Skrabala, *Planning, Programming, Budgeting, and Execution in Comparative Organizations: Vol. 2, Case Studies of Selected Allied and Partner Nations*, RAND Corporation, RR-A2195-2, 2024; Megan McKernan, Stephanie Young, Ryan Consaul, Michael Simpson, Sarah W. Denton, Anthony Vassalo, William Shelton, Devon Hill, Raphael S. Cohen, John P. Godges, Heidi Peters, and Lauren Skrabala, *Planning, Programming, Budgeting, and Execution in Comparative Organizations: Vol. 3, Case Studies of Selected Non-DoD Federal Agencies*, RAND Corporation, RR-A2195-3, 2024.

[5] Megan McKernan, Stephanie Young, Timothy R. Heath, Dara Massicot, Andrew Dowse, Devon Hill, James Black, Ryan Consaul, Michael Simpson, Sarah W. Denton, Anthony Vassalo, Ivana Ke, Mark Stalczynski, Benjamin J. Sacks, Austin Wyatt, Jade Yeung, Nicolas Jouan, Yuliya Shokh, William Shelton, Raphael S. Cohen, John P. Godges, Heidi Peters, and Lauren Skrabala, *Planning, Programming, Budgeting, and Execution in Comparative Organizations: Vol. 4, Executive Summary*, RAND Corporation, RR-A2195-4, 2024.

[6] An oft-quoted assertion by Secretary McNamara from April 20, 1963, which is pertinent to this discussion, is that "[y]ou cannot make decisions simply by asking yourself whether something might be nice to have. You have to make a judgment on how much is enough" (as cited in the introduction of Alain C. Enthoven and K. Wayne Smith, *How Much Is Enough? Shaping the Defense Program, 1961–1969*, RAND Corporation, CB-403, 1971).

together.[7] As Charles Hitch, Secretary McNamara's first comptroller and a key intellectual leader in the development and implementation of the PPBS, noted, "There is no budget size or cost that is correct regardless of the payoff, and there is no need that should be met regardless of cost."[8]

To make decisions about prioritization and where to take risk in a resource-constrained environment, DoD needed an analytic basis for making choices. Therefore, the PPBS first introduced the program budget, an *output*-oriented articulation of the resources associated with a given military capability projected over five years.[9] Second, the PPBS introduced an approach for assessing cost-effectiveness, termed *systems analysis,* which was institutionalized in an Office of Systems Analysis. Since 2009, this office has been known as Cost Assessment and Program Evaluation (CAPE).[10] At its inception, the PPBS was a process for explicitly linking resources to strategy and for setting up a structure for making explicit choices between options, based on the transparent analysis of costs and effectiveness. Then, as today, the system introduced friction with other key stakeholders, including Congress and industry partners. Key features of the PPBS have become institutionalized in DoD's PPBE System, and questions have arisen about whether its processes and structures remain relevant and agile enough to serve their intended purposes.[11]

To set up the discussion of case studies, it will be helpful to outline the key features of the PPBE process and clarify some definitions. Figure 1.1 offers a summary view of the process.

Today, consideration of PPBE often broadly encapsulates internal DoD processes, other executive branch functions, and congressional rules governing appropriations. Internal to DoD, PPBE is an annual process by which the department determines how to align strategic guidance to military programs and resources. The process supports the development of DoD inputs to the President's Budget and to a budgeting program with a five-year time hori-

---

[7] Or, as Bernard Brodie stated succinctly, "strategy wears a dollar sign" (Bernard Brodie, *Strategy in the Missile Age,* RAND Corporation, CB-137-1, 1959, p. 358).

[8] Charles J. Hitch and Roland N. McKean, *The Economics of Defense in the Nuclear Age,* RAND Corporation, R-346, 1960, p. 47.

[9] On the need for an output-oriented budget formulation at the appropriate level to make informed choices, Hitch and McKean (1960, p. 50) noted that the consumer "cannot judge intelligently how much he should spend on a car if he asks, 'How much should I devote to fenders, to steering activities, and to carburetion?' Nor can he improve his decisions much by lumping all living into a single program and asking, 'How much should I spend on life?'"

[10] In an essential treatise on the PPBS's founding, Enthoven (the first director of the Office of Systems Analysis) and Smith describe "the basic ideas that served as the intellectual foundation for PPBS" (1971, pp. 33–47) and, thus, PPBE: (1) decisionmaking should be made on explicit criteria of the national interest, (2) needs and costs should be considered together, (3) alternatives should be explicitly considered, (4) an active analytic staff should be used, (5) a multiyear force and financial plan should project consequences into the future, and (6) open and explicit analysis should form the basis for major decisions.

[11] Greenwalt and Patt, 2021, pp. 9–10.

FIGURE 1.1

DoD's PPBE Process (as of September 2019)

Fiscal Year (FY)	FY 2019	FY 2020	FY 2021	FY 2022
	O N D J F M A M J J A S	O N D J F M A M J J A S	O N D J F M A M J J A S	O N D J F M A M J J A S
FY 2020-2024	Prgm'ing/ Bdgt'ing — Congressional Enactment	Execution		
FY 2021-2025	Planning	Prgm'ing/ Bdgt'ing — Congressional Enactment	Execution	
FY 2022-2026		Planning	Prgm'ing/ Bdgt'ing — Congressional Enactment	Execution
FY 2023-2027			Planning	Prgm'ing/ Bdgt'ing — Congressional Enactment
FY 2024-2028		Time now		Planning

(Row label at left: Budget Cycles)

Planning Phase	Programming/Budgeting Phase	Congressional Enactment Process	Execution Phase
Objective Identify and prioritize future capabilities needed as a result of strategies and guidance	**Objective** Identify, balance and justify resources for requirements to complete national strategies and comply with laws and guidance	**Objective** Create laws that authorize programs and functions and appropriates the associated budget authority for execution	**Objective** Execute authorized programs and functions with appropriated resources
Key Products NSS, NDS, NMS, DPG	**Key Products** BES, POM, CPA, PBDs, PDMs, RMDs, PB	**Key Products** CBR, NDAA, Appropriations Acts, CRs	**Key Products** Obligations and expenditures (contracts, MIPRs, military pay, civilian pay, travel, GPC transactions), outlays, spend plans
Key Stakeholders President OSD JCS OUSD(A&S) SECDEF OUSD(P) COCOMs OUSD(R&E) OMB DoD Components	**Key Stakeholders** President OSD CAPE JCS OUSD(C) SECDEF OUSD(A&S) COCOMs OUSD(R&E) OMB DoD Components OSD	**Key Stakeholders** Congress (Committees and Subcommittees) President SECDEF COCOMs DoD Components	**Key Stakeholders** Treasury OUSD(R&E) GAO DoD Components OMB DFAS OUSD(C) Industry Partners OUSD(A&S)

SOURCE: Reproduced from Stephen Speciale and Wayne B. Sullivan II, "DoD Financial Management—More Money, More Problems," Defense Acquisition University, September 1, 2019, p. 6.

NOTE: BES = budget estimation submission; CBR = concurrent budget resolution; COCOM = combatant command; CPA = Chairperson's Program Assessment; CR = continuing resolution; DFAS = Defense Finance and Accounting Services; DPG = defense planning guidance; GAO = U.S. Government Accountability Office; GPC = government purchase card; JCS = Joint Chiefs of Staff; MIPR = military interdepartmental purchase request; NDAA = National Defense Authorization Act; NDS = National Defense Strategy; NMS = National Military Strategy; NSS = National Security Strategy; OMB = Office of Management and Budget; OSD = Office of the Secretary of Defense; OUSD(A&S) = Office of the Under Secretary of Defense (Acquisition and Sustainment); OUSD(C) = Office of the Under Secretary of Defense (Comptroller); OUSD(P) = Office of the Under Secretary of Defense (Policy); OUSD(R&E) = Office of the Under Secretary of Defense (Research and Engineering); PB = President's Budget; PBD = program budget decision; PDM = program decision memorandum; POM = program objective memorandum; RMD = resource management decision; SECDEF = Secretary of Defense.

zon, known as the Future Years Defense Program (FYDP).[12] DoD Directive (DoDD) 7045.14, *The Planning, Programming, Budgeting, and Execution (PPBE) Process*, states that one intent for PPBE "is to provide the DOD with the most effective mix of forces, equipment, man-

---

[12] Brendan W. McGarry, *Defense Primer: Planning, Programming, Budgeting and Execution (PPBE) Process*, Congressional Research Service, IF10429, January 27, 2020, p. 1.

power, and support attainable within fiscal constraints."[13] PPBE consists of four distinct processes, each with its own outputs and stakeholders. Select objectives of each phase include the following:

- **Planning:** "Integrate assessments of potential military threats facing the country, overall national strategy and defense policy, ongoing defense plans and programs, and projected financial resources into an overall statement of policy."[14]
- **Programming:** "[A]nalyze the anticipated effects of present-day decisions on the future force" and detail the specific forces and programs proposed over the FYDP period to meet the military requirements identified in the plans and within the financial limits.[15]
- **Budgeting:** "[E]nsure appropriate funding and fiscal controls, phasing of the efforts over the funding period, and feasibility of execution within the budget year"; restructure budget categories for submission to Congress according to the appropriation accounts; and prepare justification material for submission to Congress.[16]
- **Execution:** "[D]etermine how well programs and financing have met joint warfighting needs."[17]

Several features of congressional appropriations processes are particularly important to note. First, since fiscal year 1960, Congress has provided budget authority to DoD through specific appropriations titles (sometimes termed *colors of money*), the largest of which are operation and maintenance (O&M); military personnel; research, development, test, and evaluation (RDT&E); and procurement.[18] These appropriations titles are further broken down into *appropriation accounts*, such as Military Personnel, Army or Shipbuilding and Conversion, Navy (SCN). Second, the budget authority provided in one of these accounts is generally available for obligation only within a specified period. In the DoD budget, the period of availability for military personnel and O&M accounts is one year; for RDT&E accounts, two years; and for most procurement accounts, three years (although for SCN, it can be five or six years, in certain circumstances). This specification means that budget authority must be obligated within those periods or, with only a few exceptions, it is lost.[19] There has been recent interest

---

[13] DoDD 7045.14, *The Planning, Programming, Budgeting, and Execution (PPBE) Process*, U.S. Department of Defense, August 29, 2017, p. 2.

[14] Congressional Research Service, *A Defense Budget Primer*, RL30002, December 9, 1998, p. 27.

[15] Congressional Research Service, 1998, p. 27; McGarry, 2020, p. 2.

[16] McGarry, 2020, p. 2; Congressional Research Service, 1998, p. 28.

[17] DoDD 7045.14, 2017, p. 11.

[18] Congressional Research Service, 1998, pp. 15–17.

[19] Congressional Research Service, 1998, pp. 49–50. Regarding RDT&E, see U.S. Code, Title 10, Section 3131, Availability of Appropriations.

in exploring how these features of the appropriations process affect transparency and oversight, institutional incentives, and the exercise of flexibility, should resource needs change.[20]

Importantly, PPBE touches almost everything DoD does and, thus, forms a critical touchpoint for engagement with stakeholders across DoD (e.g., OSD, military departments, Joint Staff, COCOMs), in the executive branch (through OMB), in Congress, and among industry partners.

Research Approach and Methods

In close partnership with the commission, we selected nine case studies to explore decisionmaking in organizations facing challenges similar to those experienced in DoD: exercising agility in the face of changing needs and enabling innovation. Two near-peer case studies were specifically called for in the legislation, in part to allow the commission to explore the competitiveness implications of strategic adversaries' approaches to resource planning.

For all nine case studies, we conducted extensive document reviews and structured discussions with subject-matter experts having experience in the budgeting processes of the international governments and other U.S. federal government agencies. For case studies of two allied and partner countries, the team leveraged the expertise of researchers in RAND Europe (located in Cambridge, United Kingdom) and RAND Australia (located in Canberra, Australia) with direct experience in partner defense organizations. Given the diversity in subject-matter expertise required across the case studies, each one was assigned a unique team with appropriate regional or organizational expertise. For the near-peer competitor cases, the assigned experts had the language skills and methodological training to facilitate working with primary sources in Chinese or Russian. The analysis was also supplemented by experts in PPBE as applicable.

Case study research drew primarily on government documentation outlining processes and policies, planning guidance, budget documentation, and published academic and policy research. Although participants in structured discussions varied in accordance with the decisionmaking structures across case studies, they generally included chief financial officers, representatives from organizations responsible for making programmatic choices, and budget officials. For obvious reasons, the China and Russia case studies faced unique challenges in data collection and in identifying and accessing interview targets with direct knowledge of PPBE-like processes.

To facilitate consistency, completeness in addressing the commission's highest-priority areas of interest, and cross-case comparisons, the team developed a common case study template. This template took specific questions from the commission as several inputs, aligned key questions to PPBE processes and oversight mechanisms, evaluated perceived strengths and challenges of each organization's processes and their applicability to DoD processes, and

---

[20] McGarry, 2022.

concluded with lessons learned from each case. To enable the development of a more consistent evidentiary base across cases, the team also developed a standard interview protocol to guide the structured discussions.

Areas of Focus

Given the complexity of PPBE and its many connections to other processes and stakeholders, along with other inputs and ongoing analysis by the commission, we needed to scope this work in accordance with three of the commission's top priorities.

First, although we sought insights across PPBE phases in each case study, in accordance with the commission's guidance, we placed a particular emphasis on an organization's budgeting and execution mechanisms, such as the existence of appropriations titles (i.e., colors of money), and on any mechanisms for exercising flexibility, such as reprogramming thresholds. However, it is important to note that this level of detailed information was not uniformly available. The opacity of internal processes in China and Russia made the budget mechanisms much more difficult to discern in those cases in particular.

Second, while the overall investment portfolios varied in accordance with varying mission needs, the case studies were particularly focused on investments related to RDT&E and procurement rather than O&M or sustainment activities.

Third, the case studies of other U.S. federal government agencies did not focus primarily on the roles played by external stakeholders, such as OMB, Congress, and industry partners. Such stakeholders were discussed when relevant insights emerged from other sources, but interviews and data collection were focused within the bounds of a given organization rather than across a broader network of key stakeholders.

Research Limitations and Caveats

This research required detailed analysis of the nuances of internal resource planning processes across nine extraordinarily diverse organizations and on a tight timeline required by the commission's challenging mandate. This breadth of scope was intended to provide the commission with diverse insights into how other organizations address similar challenges but also limited the depth the team could pursue for any one case. These constraints warrant additional discussion of research limitations and caveats of two types.

First, each case study, to a varying degree, confronted limitations in data availability. The teams gathered documentation from publicly available sources and doggedly pursued additional documentation from targeted interviews and other experts with direct experience, but even for the cases from allied countries and U.S. federal agencies, including DoD, there was a limit to what could be established in formal documentation. Some important features of how systems work in practice are not captured in formal documentation, and such features had to be teased out and triangulated from interviews to the extent that appropriate officials were available to engage with the team. The general opacity and lack of institutional connections to decisionmakers in China and Russia introduced unique challenges for data collection.

Russia was further obscured by the war in Ukraine during the research period, which made access by U.S.-based researchers to reliable government data on current plans and resource allocation impossible.

Second, the case study teams confronted important inconsistencies across cases, which made cross-case comparability very challenging to establish. For example, international cases each involved unique political cultures, governance structures, strategic concerns, and military commitments—all of which we characterize to the extent that it is essential context for understanding how and why resource allocation decisions are made. The context-dependent nature of the international cases made even defining the "defense budget" difficult, given countries' various definitions and inclusions. With respect to the near-peer case studies of China and Russia presented in this report, inconsistencies were especially pronounced regarding the purchasing power within those two countries. To address some of these inconsistencies, we referenced the widely cited Stockholm International Peace Research Institute (SIPRI) Military Expenditure Database.[21] With respect to the other U.S. federal agencies, each agency had its own unique mission, organizational culture, resource level, and process of congressional oversight—all of which were critical for understanding how and why resource allocation decisions were made. This diversity strained our efforts to draw cross-case comparisons or to develop internally consistent normative judgments of best practices. For this reason, each case study analysis and articulation of strengths and challenges should be understood relative to each organization's *own* unique resource allocation needs and missions.

Near-Peer Competitors Focus

The 2022 National Defense Strategy (NDS) describes a security environment of complex strategic challenges associated with such dynamics as emerging technology, transboundary threats, and competitors posing "new threats to the U.S. homeland and to strategic stability."[22] Among these challenges, the NDS notes that "[t]he most comprehensive and serious challenge" is the People's Republic of China (PRC). The NDS points to China's military modernization and exercise of whole-of-government levers to effect "coercive" and "aggressive" approaches to the region and international order.[23] Although the NDS designates China as the "pacing challenge" for DoD, it also highlights the threat posed by Russia as an "acute threat."[24]

To better understand and operate in the competitive environment, the Commission on PPBE Reform is considering "budgeting methodologies and strategies of near-peer competi-

---

[21] SIPRI, "SIPRI Military Expenditure Database," homepage, undated.

[22] DoD, *2022 National Defense Strategy of the United States of America*, 2022, p. 4.

[23] DoD, 2022, p. 4.

[24] DoD, 2022, pp. 4–5.

tors to understand if and how such competitors can address current and future threats more or less successfully than the United States."[25] Notably, this focus on internal processes as key enablers of military outcomes is well aligned to the NDS's imperative to "build enduring advantage," "undertak[e] reforms to accelerate force development, [get] the technology we need more quickly, and mak[e] investments in the extraordinary people of the Department, who remain our most valuable resource."[26] This imperative has prompted reflection on the extent to which internal DoD processes, including PPBE, are up to the challenge of enabling rapid and responsive capability development to address the emerging threats.

China

China's rise from a technologically backward and poorly equipped military in the 1970s to the U.S. pacing challenge in 2022 has made it a case study of particular interest to DoD policymakers with regard to the apparent drivers of relative comparative advantage. China's military modernization is especially remarkable given the speed with which it has occurred.

In 1979, Beijing abandoned Maoist economic policies in favor of more-pragmatic, market-friendly reforms. In the 1980s, the country prioritized rapid economic growth, and military modernization progressed slowly. However, over the following decade, the defense budget soared. From 2000 to 2016, China's military budget increased annually by about 10 percent, although this growth has slowed to about 5–7 percent per year.[27]

Figure 1.2 illustrates the steady rise in China's military expenditure over time; however, estimating the actual size of China's defense budget has remained difficult because of Beijing's lack of transparency and the country's incomplete transition to a market economy. According to government sources, China's defense budget was $230 billion in 2022, second only to that of the United States.[28] Years of major budget increases have yielded an increasingly lethal and capable People's Liberation Army (PLA). As we describe in detail in Chapter 2, the story of China's recent military successes is difficult to disentangle from the country's broader story of economic development, the sheer scale of increased investment in the military, workforce development, the development of advanced manufacturing and industrial capabilities, and other transformative social and economic factors. This is a case, it might be argued, for which the ruling leaders of the Chinese Community Party (CCP) have made substantial and sustained investment in building enduring advantage.[29]

What has enabled China's achievements in the science and technological innovation underlying military modernization? Analysts have pointed to several contributing factors.

[25] Public Law 117–81, 2021, Section 1004(f)(2)(F).

[26] DoD, 2022, p. iv.

[27] Defense Intelligence Agency, *China Military Power: Modernizing a Force to Fight and Win*, 2019, p. 20.

[28] Zhao Lei, "China to Raise Military Budget by 7.1% This Year," *China Daily*, March 6, 2022.

[29] For a broader look at factors associated with a country's competitive posture, see Michael J. Mazarr, *The Societal Foundations of National Competitiveness*, RAND Corporation, RR-A499-1, 2022.

FIGURE 1.2
Military Expenditures, by Country, 1993–2021

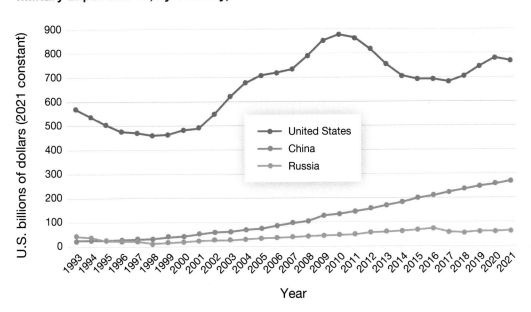

SOURCE: Features information from SIPRI, "SIPRI Military Expenditure Database," homepage, undated. Data shown are as of March 17, 2023.

China's technological innovations build on the advantages of the country's industrial base. China has a large manufacturing capacity, ample mineral resources, and a strong science and technology sector.[30] China's science and technology workforce has grown dramatically, and government spending on research and development has grown at a compounding annual rate of 15 percent since 2010.[31] An analysis of China's innovation-related capabilities has noted steady improvements over time, owing to the combined effects of a more educated workforce, strong manufacturing capacity, investments in infrastructure to support scientific and technological research and development, technology transfer, and gains from civil-military technological collaboration.[32] Technology transfer in China focuses in part on U.S. and Western technologies that are transferred or stolen by China's PLA, state-owned enterprises (SOEs), or other enterprises, which has helped decrease the time needed to build capabilities. Indeed,

[30] Cortney Weinbaum, Caolionn O'Connell, Steven W. Popper, M. Scott Bond, Hannah Jane Byrne, Christian Curriden, Gregory Weider Fauerbach, Sale Lilly, Jared Mondschein, and Jon Schmid, *Assessing Systemic Strengths and Vulnerabilities of China's Defense Industrial Base: With a Repeatable Methodology for Other Countries*, RAND Corporation, RR-A930-1, 2022.

[31] Mark Ashby, Caolionn O'Connell, Edward Geist, Jair Aguirre, Christian Curriden, and Jonathan Fujiwara, *Defense Acquisition in Russia and China*, RAND Corporation, RR-A113-1, 2021, p. 24.

[32] Tai-Ming Cheung, *Innovate to Dominate: The Rise of the Chinese Techno-Security State*, Cornell University Press, 2022.

part of what has enabled China's rapid achievements is intellectual property theft from the West, including the siphoning of U.S. scientific research.[33]

China's military budgeting practices could also play a role in its military's successes in research and development and technological innovation. Beijing's emphasis on long-term strategic planning and the ability to allocate resources to projects deemed nationally important could contribute to the country's sustained investments in priority technologies. However, given the uneven successes in China's technological pursuits, the role of budget practices likely remains secondary to more critical factors related to the maturity of relevant industrial sectors.

Russia

Russia is 30 years past a painful transition from a Soviet planned economy to a partially market-based economy. Although Russia has largely left its Soviet planning model in the past, it has carried forward certain ideas and legacies of centralized economic control. For example, in Russia, competition between defense firms is not viewed as an inherently good thing that could spur innovation and increase productivity. Instead, it is viewed as a mechanism that dilutes available funds. State ownership is viewed as protection from international markets and sanctions and as a mechanism to keep unproductive companies afloat.

Russia can be fiscally conservative at the federal level, avoiding deficits and engaging in little foreign borrowing, and its defense acquisition plans are often closely tied to military strategy and defense needs. However, opacity in multiple parts of Russia's PPBE-like process, even within Russia—compounded by insufficient oversight—often perpetuates corruption and generates outputs of varying quality from the defense industry.

Russian leaders realize that their defense budget is limited and that they are outspent by their rivals; they speak often about their desire for a modern, capable military.[34] Although there have been attempts to reduce systemic graft and corruption in the past decade, the war in Ukraine has revealed these efforts to be insufficient.[35] The desire for a well-oiled defense industrial base often collides with the excessive concentration of power in Russia's executive branch and the informal practices that make business possible in modern Russia.

An understanding of Russia's defense industrial base is essential for understanding Russia's military resource decisionmaking. Russia's defense industrial base comprises approximately 800 companies or entities with a workforce of nearly 3 million, consolidated under

---

[33] Weinbaum et al., 2022, p. 19.

[34] "NATO's Military Spending Exceeds Russian Army Budget by 20 Times, Says Security Chief," Tass, June 24, 2021.

[35] Guy Anderson, "Russia Introduces Legislation to Crack Down on Defence Corruption," *Janes Defence Industry*, October 13, 2016; "The Military Prosecutor Called Theft in the Ministry of Defense 'Cosmic'" ["Военный прокурор назвал воровство в Минобороны «космическим»"], Lenta.ru, January 11, 2012.

partial or majority state ownership.[36] Consolidation began under a federal program known as Reform and Development of the Defense Industrial Complex, 2002–2006, which was motivated by a desire to vertically integrate various design, development, and manufacturing entities with a focus on distinct domains, in contrast to Soviet-era organizational structures.[37] After 2007, Russia consolidated most of its defense firms under state control to protect them on the global market, create efficiencies in Russia, and ensure more-direct oversight to account for funds and reduce graft.

Although consolidating firms under state control has generated efficiencies, the consolidation and protectionist policies have also stymied innovation, given the lack of domestic competition. Furthermore, corruption has long plagued Russia's defense industry and its government more broadly. In 2012, Russian and Western analysts estimated that 20–40 percent of annual funding from the State Defense Order (SDO) for military procurement was lost because of corruption, inflated prices for military goods, or the use of earmarked allocations for other purposes.[38] These findings led to various reforms: imposing larger fines and criminal penalties on individuals and organizations, moving responsibility for the SDO to the Russian Ministry of Defense (MoD), and paying defense industry entities through restricted accounts at state-owned banks.[39]

However, as evidenced by the 2022 war in Ukraine, corruption persists in Russia's defense industrial base. Official accounts from the United States and unofficial reports from Ukrainian and Russian social media have revealed a Russian Army that lacks appropriate equipment, logistics, and even first-aid kits.[40] Observers have documented Russian equipment without its necessary defensive components, including missing or hollowed-out explosive reactive armor on T-80 battle tanks.[41] Transparency International, a nonprofit research, monitoring, and advocacy organization, attributes the high incidence of corruption in Russia's defense indus-

---

[36] Janes, "Defence Industry Country Overview: Russian Federation," *Janes World Defence Industry*, November 17, 2022b.

[37] Janes, 2022b. Under the Soviet model, production of systems was purposefully dispersed across Russia to preserve capabilities in the event of war, whereas the post-Soviet reforms were meant to focus production at entities with the strongest potential for further development in their domains in a market economy (Julian Cooper, "Transforming Russia's Defense Industrial Base," *Survival*, Vol. 35, No. 4, Winter 1993).

[38] Anderson, 2016; "The Military Prosecutor Called Theft in the Ministry of Defense 'Cosmic'" ["Военный прокурор назвал воровство в Минобороны «космическим»"], 2012. The SDO is known as the *Gosudarstvennyy oborony zakaz*, or GOZ, in Russian.

[39] Anderson, 2016.

[40] Sam Cranny-Evans and Olga Ivshina, "Corruption in the Russian Armed Forces," Royal United Services Institute, May 12, 2022; Polina Beliakova, "Russian Military's Corruption Quagmire," *Politico*, March 8, 2022; Mark Schneider, "Lessons from Russian Missile Performance in Ukraine," *Proceedings*, Vol. 148/10/1436, October 2022; Rob Lee [@RALee85], "Photos comparing Ukrainian (below) and inferior Russian (above) first aid kits posted by Russian sources," post on the X platform, April 29, 2022.

[41] Paul D. Shinkman, "How Russian Corruption Is Foiling Putin's Army in Ukraine," *U.S. News and World Report*, August 31, 2022.

trial base to a lack of external, transparent oversight of PPBE-like functions—specifically, oversight over the functions of defense policy, budgeting, and acquisition.[42]

Structure of This Report

In Chapter 2, we provide a detailed case study of China's defense resource planning, followed by Chapter 3, in which we provide a case study of Russia's defense resource planning. In Chapter 4, we review key insights across the two case studies.

---

[42] Transparency International Defence and Security, "Russia," Government Defence Integrity Index 2020, June 2019–May 2020.

China

Timothy Heath and Ivana Ke

China's military budget is the overall budget allocated by the central government for the armed forces of China, known as the PLA.[1] The PLA is one of the largest militaries in the world, with responsibilities to uphold CCP rule; protect China's sovereignty and territorial claims, including contested maritime and land borders; deter and defeat Taiwan separatism; and protect China's overseas interests.[2] Senior U.S. officials have described the PLA as the U.S. military's pacing challenge.[3]

The PLA's main services are a ground force (PLA Ground Force), navy (PLA Navy), air force (PLA Air Force), nuclear and conventional missile force (PLA Rocket Force), and the PLA Strategic Support Force, which is responsible for providing cyber, space, surveillance, reconnaissance, and information support. The PLA has about 2 million personnel and fields a technologically advanced military equipped with stealth fighters (J-20s), aircraft carriers, hypersonic missiles (DF-17s), nuclear submarines, and other sophisticated platforms and weapons.[4]

China's military modernization is especially remarkable given the speed with which it has occurred. In 1979, Beijing abandoned Maoist economic policies in favor of more-pragmatic, market-friendly reforms. At that time, the PLA was a technologically backward, poorly equipped military. In the 1980s, the country prioritized rapid economic growth, and military modernization progressed slowly. However, over the following decade, Chinese leaders elevated defense spending, and the defense budget soared. From 2000 to 2016, China's military budget increased annually by about 10 percent, although this growth subsequently slowed to about 5–7 percent per year (Figure 2.1).[5] According to PRC government sources, China's

---

[1] China's local governments provide some resources to support the military in the form of provincial military base operating costs. However, in this study, we focused on the central government budget for defense spending.

[2] Defense Intelligence Agency, 2019.

[3] Jim Garamone, "Official Talks DoD Policy Role in Chinese Pacing Threat, Integrated Deterrence Role," U.S. Department of Defense, June 2, 2021.

[4] Defense Intelligence Agency, 2019.

[5] Defense Intelligence Agency, 2019, p. 20.

FIGURE 2.1

China's Official Defense Spending, 2007–2018

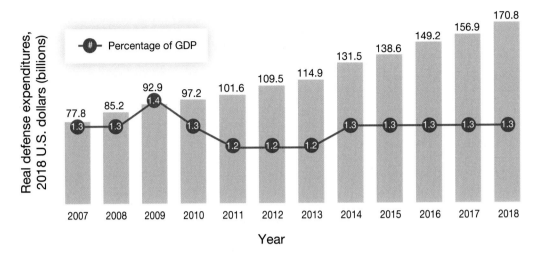

SOURCE: Adapted from Defense Intelligence Agency, 2019, p. 21.
NOTE: Numbers inside circles represent the percentage of China's gross domestic product (GDP).

defense budget was $230 billion in 2022, second only to that of the United States.[6] By contrast, in 2003, the PLA's official budget was about $22 billion.[7]

Estimating the actual size of China's defense budget has remained difficult because of Beijing's lack of transparency and the country's incomplete transition to a market economy. China provides explanations of spending categories to the United Nations and in defense white papers that are published biennially. According to these sources, the budget consists of three roughly equal categories of spending: equipment, personnel, and training and mainte-nance.[8] However, experts have pointed out that official budgets omit key categories of spend-ing, such as paramilitary forces, provincial base operating costs, and certain categories of defense-related research and development. Research conducted by Western think tanks, such as SIPRI and the Institute for International Strategic Studies, suggests that the difference could amount to $65 billion per year.[9] This difference is further magnified when considering military purchasing power parity (PPP). One study, for instance, has found that China's 2017

---

[6] Zhao, 2022.

[7] Willy Wo-Lap Lam, "Budget Surprise for China's Army," CNN, March 6, 2003.

[8] State Council Information Office of the People's Republic of China, *China's National Defense in the New Era*, June 24, 2019; United Nations Office for Disarmament Affairs, "Military Expenditures Database," web-page, undated.

[9] Nan Tian and Fei Su, *A New Estimate of China's Military Expenditure*, Stockholm International Peace Research Institute, January 2021; Meia Nouwens and Lucie Béraud-Sudreau, *Assessing Chinese Defence Spending: Proposals for New Methodologies*, Institute for International Strategic Studies, March 2020.

military budget could have been as high as $393.6 billion in military PPP terms. However, scholars continue to dispute how much of China's military spending can be reasonably compared using PPP calculations.[10]

Years of major budget increases have yielded an increasingly lethal and capable PLA. Military analysts have pointed out that China's formidable array of long-range missiles, modern warships, advanced sensors, and other weapons pose an increasingly serious threat to U.S. forces that might intervene in a conflict near Taiwan. As early as 2015, RAND Corporation researchers warned of a "receding frontier of U.S. dominance," noting that China's military had "narrowed the gap" in capabilities with the U.S. military.[11] U.S. officials have steadily warned of an eroding military advantage in the face of rapid PLA gains.[12]

In 2017, the CCP adopted the goal of transforming the PLA into a world-class military by 2049, in part by leveraging civilian technologies through a "military-civil fusion" initiative.[13] China's success in developing advanced military technologies at a faster rate than the United States has underscored the enormous achievements of China's defense industry. Notably, the PLA's recent successes in launching hypersonic glide vehicles have elicited concerns that China's system has an advantage when it comes to developing and deploying advanced military capabilities.[14]

The PLA's astonishing speed of modernization, the relative decline in U.S. military advantage, and a deepening of U.S.-China tensions have led many to question how China has managed to improve its ability to innovate in such a brief time. Analysts have noted many contributing factors to China's achievements in science and technological innovation. For example, China's research community, backed by state resources, has focused on key technology areas, such as blockchain, enabling early successes.[15] China's technological innovations also build on the advantages of the country's industrial base. China has a large manufacturing capacity, ample mineral resources, and a strong science and technology sector.[16] China's

---

[10] Peter E. Robertson, "The Real Military Balance: International Comparisons of Defense Spending," *Review of Income and Wealth*, Vol. 68, No. 3, September 2022.

[11] Eric Heginbotham, Michael Nixon, Forrest E. Morgan, Jacob L. Heim, Jeff Hagen, Sheng Tao Li, Jeffrey Engstrom, Martin C. Libicki, Paul DeLuca, David A. Shlapak, David R. Frelinger, Burgess Laird, Kyle Brady, and Lyle J. Morris, *The U.S.-China Military Scorecard: Forces, Geography, and the Evolving Balance of Power, 1996–2017*, RAND Corporation, RR-392-AF, 2015, pp. xxxi, iii.

[12] Robert Burns, "Pentagon Rattled by Chinese Military Push on Multiple Fronts," Associated Press, November 1, 2021.

[13] "Full Text of Xi Jinping's Report at the 19th CPC Congress," Xinhua, November 3, 2017.

[14] Demetri Sevastopulo and Kathrin Hille, "China Tests New Space Capability with Hypersonic Missile," *Financial Times*, October 16, 2021.

[15] Steven W. Popper, Marjory S. Blumenthal, Eugeniu Han, Sale Lilly, Lyle J. Morris, Caroline S. Wagner, Christopher A. Eusebi, Brian G. Carlson, and Alice Shih, *China's Propensity for Innovation in the 21st Century: Identifying Indicators of Future Outcomes*, RAND Corporation, RR-A208-1, 2020.

[16] Weinbaum et al., 2022.

science and technology workforce has increased dramatically, and government spending on research and development has grown at a compounding annual rate of 15 percent since 2010.[17] According to a 2021 RAND report, these foundations and investments put China on a path to "mitigating some of its historical shortcomings in [research, development, and acquisition] execution."[18] An analysis of China's innovation-related capabilities also noted steady improvements over time, owing to the combined effects of a more educated workforce, strong manufacturing capacity, investments in infrastructure to support scientific and technological research and development, technology transfer, and gains from civil-military technological collaboration.[19]

China's budgeting practices for the military likely played a limited role at most in its military's successes in research and development and technological innovation. Beijing's emphasis on long-term strategic planning and the ability to allocate resources to projects deemed nationally important could contribute to sustained investments in priority technologies. However, China's budgeting practices have not changed dramatically over the past 20 years and are generally regarded as lagging behind those of its Western counterparts. China employs outdated budgeting practices and suffers from weak accountability, corruption, and inefficiency. Accordingly, Chinese officials have long sought to imitate some practices commonly used in Western countries to improve their government's ability to execute budgets. In sum, factors other than China's budget process likely have played more-important roles in driving the country's successes in military modernization. Nevertheless, an understanding of China's defense budget process can help illuminate the ways in which the PLA's approach to military spending facilitates or impedes its overall modernization efforts.

Aware of the challenges of its budgeting and financial system, the PLA has frequently sought to reform its system.[20] Many of the system's problems stem from the country's adherence to outdated centralized budgetary practices in which most economic decisions are made by high-level government authorities instead of market participants. For example, ministries and subnational governments in China have relied extensively on extrabudgetary revenues, which are public resources raised by authorities through methods not included in the annual budget and thus not subject to the same level of regulation and audit. These methods tend to consist of fines, sales of public goods (e.g., land and mining rights), and other fees. Because of the lack of reporting and oversight, extrabudgetary revenues lend themselves to corruption and soft budget constraints. For decades, China's subnational governments also relied on a form of cash-based accounting that Western governments abandoned in the 1970s in favor

---

[17] Ashby et al., 2021, p. 24.

[18] Ashby et al., 2021, p. 31.

[19] Cheung, 2022.

[20] Jia Shiyu, "The Central Military Commission Approves the Implementation of Military Performance Management" ["中央军委批准推行军费绩效管理"], *People's Daily*, October 27, 2014.

of a more accurate accrual-based approach.[21] Accrual-based accounting is more complex, but it provides a more accurate picture of expenses and income because it requires budgetary authorities to record when transactions are made, not when cash is received or spent. This method makes it easier to track budgets more accurately and is generally accepted as the norm for larger businesses and government bureaucracies. PLA scholarly writings suggest that, although China's military finance system has improved, there are still issues with inefficient spending, transparency, and accountability. These sources occasionally suggest that the PLA study and learn from Western PPBE practices—and that China's military scholars *are* learning from the perceived strengths and challenges of these practices.[22]

To improve accountability, reduce waste, and control corruption, the CCP has carried out numerous government budgeting reforms. The latest initiative occurred as part of the broader reform agenda promoted at the Third Plenum of the 18th Party Congress, which was held in 2013. In 2014, the government passed its Budget Law, which sought to streamline funding sources, eliminate extrabudgetary revenues, improve transparency and accountability, and standardize procedures.[23] The law directed departments and ministries at all levels to adopt a multiyear budget to better support planning and management of fiscal policy. Crucially, the law allowed subnational governments to issue bonds to finance fiscal expenditures and thus shut down off-budget revenue-raising activities by local governments, such as sales of public lands to developers.[24] The PLA dutifully developed regulations and policies to implement the Budget Law in subsequent years.

In the next three sections of this case study, we offer an overview of China's defense budgeting process (its decisionmakers and stakeholders, planning and programming, budgeting and execution, and oversight), an analysis of China's defense budgeting practices (its strengths, challenges, and applicability to DoD's PPBE system), and lessons from China's defense budgeting process. A concluding section closes the chapter.

However, the findings below need to be understood in light of the research limitations. Our research relies primarily on Western scholarly research and Chinese news articles and journal publications. China's defense budget has spurred considerable commentary and analysis in recent decades, but scholarship on the details of the military's budget process has remained scarce. The last major study, led by Dennis Blasko, was published in 2006,

---

[21] Gouhua Hang, "China Moves Ahead on Accrual Accounting," *IMF Public Financial Management Blog*, December 4, 2015.

[22] Huai Fuli et al., "An Analysis of the Feasibility of Using PPBES as a Reference for Our Country's National Defense Budget System Reform" ["我国国防预算制度改革借鉴PPBES的可行性分析"], *Military Economics Research* [军事经济研究], July 2015. See Annex A of that article for a full analysis of the perceived strengths and challenges of China's system in implementing a PPBE-like approach to budget formulation. See also Ding Zhaozhong and Li Zhaochun, "Research on PPBE Defense Budget System Reform with Chinese Characteristics" ["中国特色PPBE 国防预算制度改革研究"], *Contemporary Economics* [当代经济], June 2016.

[23] "Budget Law of the People's Republic of China," Xinhua, August 31, 2014.

[24] Philippe Wingender, "Intergovernmental Fiscal Reform in China," International Monetary Fund Working Paper No. 18/88, April 13, 2018.

nearly two decades ago, when a team of experts traveled to China to interview officials on this topic.[25] Chinese-language sources that describe China's defense budget process remain extremely limited. Moreover, many of the publicly available sources that we reviewed were published before the most recent reforms, which began around 2016. Thus, we had only a limited ability to evaluate the effectiveness of recent changes to the PLA's defense budget process. In addition, the information asymmetry between the U.S. defense budgeting processes and China's presents challenges in drawing comparative findings. Consequently, readers should be wary in drawing hard conclusions about strengths and challenges of the U.S. system relative to China's system.

Overview of China's Defense Budgeting Process

In accordance with centrally directed reforms to all branches of the government, the PLA has carried out multiple rounds of reforms in its budgeting and financial system, including some that predated the 2014 Budget Law. A major change occurred in 2001, when the Central Military Commission (CMC) approved the Military Budgeting Reform Implementation Plan, which introduced zero-based, comprehensive, and classification budgeting in adherence to the central government's budget system and in accordance with internationally accepted budgeting standards.[26] The Military Accounting Rules of 2002 deepened the integration of military accounting laws with relevant state accounting laws and regulations to promote the exchange of knowledge, training, and personnel across military and civil sectors.[27]

In China's political system, changes to national state laws require all bureaucracies and ministries to comply by adapting their own respective rules and regulations. This has affected the budget process. The PLA's main budget-related reforms in the past few decades began as efforts to ensure compliance with relevant laws and regulations adopted by the central government.[28] Although few details on the inner workings of China's budgetary process can be found in the public domain, its basic steps can be deduced through an examination of available laws and reports, as reflected in Figure 2.2.

In subsequent sections of this chapter, we provide an overview of the processes through which China's military plans, develops, executes, and monitors its budgets. We begin with a

---

[25] Dennis J. Blasko, Chas W. Freeman, Jr., Stanley A. Horowitz, Evan S. Medeiros, and James C. Mulvenon, *Defense-Related Spending in China: A Preliminary Analysis and Comparison with American Equivalents,* United States–China Policy Foundation, 2006.

[26] "Military Budgeting Reform Implementation Plan," Xinhua, March 22, 2001. *Zero-based budgeting* is a method that requires all expenses to be justified and approved for each budget period, *comprehensive budgeting* includes all income and expenses, and *classification budgeting* involves coding schemes for each item in the budget.

[27] Yang Shipeng and Zeng Lingbo, "Commentary on the Focus of Military Accounting System Reforms" ["军队会计制度改革焦点评述"], *Military Economic Research* [军事经济研究], July 2006.

[28] "Chinese Army to Tighten Expenditure," Xinhua, February 24, 2013.

FIGURE 2.2

The Budgeting Process in China

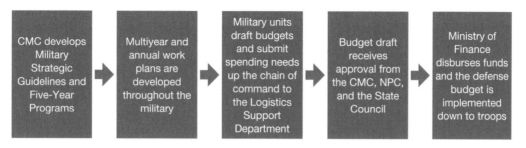

SOURCES: Features information from Susan V. Lawrence and Mari Y. Lee, *China's Political System in Charts: A Snapshot Before the 20th Party Congress*, Congressional Research Service, R46977, November 24, 2021; Blasko et al., 2006.
NOTE: NPC = National People's Congress.

review of the key decisionmakers and stakeholders before examining steps in the development and execution of China's military budget.

Decisionmakers and Stakeholders

China's decisionmaking apparatus is highly centralized yet poorly integrated across the national government's ministries. Senior CCP leaders are responsible for making the most-important decisions and addressing the most-fundamental questions of national strategy. However, there has been a lack of coordination across the ministries, often because of competing interests. This poor coordination often results in inefficiencies and redundant or conflicting policies implemented by the ministries. CCP senior leadership—which constitutes the party's real center of power—comprises the Politburo Standing Committee, consisting of the seven most senior party leaders; the Politburo, consisting of the 26 most senior officials; and the Central Committee Secretariat.

The NPC, which serves as the country's legislature and supreme authority in the government bureaucracy, reviews and formally approves the defense budget every year. It also provides a report on the previous year's budget. However, in practice, the NPC generally rubber-stamps decisions made by the CCP's central leadership. Within the NPC, a standing committee consisting of a select group of delegates carries out the body's day-to-day work. According to the 2014 Budget Law, this committee supervises the implementation of the budget, reviews and approves any adjustments, and reviews and approves the final accounts of the central government. The NPC's Finance and Economic Affairs Committee is responsible for the preliminary reviews of both the draft budget and the central government's accounts.[29]

The State Council and the PLA, in turn, translate the instructions from the central party leadership into more-detailed directives, plans, and requirements. The State Council is the

---

[29] "Budget Law of the People's Republic of China," 2014.

highest-level administrative authority in the government bureaucracy. Its job is to oversee the implementation of central party leaders' directives in the form of government policy. It also oversees the implementation of the budget as approved by the NPC. In reality, the memberships of the State Council and the Politburo overlap considerably. Within the State Council, the Ministry of Finance (MOF)—and, in particular, the National Defense Department within the MOF—plays a critical role in managing the disbursement of funds and coordinating budgeting processes with the military.[30]

The CMC plays a critical role in China's military budget. The CMC is the highest-level command organization in the military. It is responsible for examining and approving the outline for the PLA's five-year programs, long-term plans for military defense modernization, and the PLA's annual general budgets and military-wide regulations on financial work and expenditure standards.[31]

The CMC has several offices that play key roles in the military budgeting process. Its Logistics Support Department and Strategic Planning Office oversee most of the budget staff at the national level. The General Logistics Department (GLD) previously handled these responsibilities, but it was disbanded along with the three other primary CMC entities as part of the PLA's 2015 reorganization, and its budgetary duties were transferred to departments within the CMC. The Financial Bureau, part of the Logistics Support Department, plays an important role in developing finance-related regulations. In 2016, the CMC established the Auditing Office to strengthen oversight of the military's budget and financial departments.[32]

Entities outside the CMC also play important roles. CCP committees comprising PLA officers and technical experts who are also party members govern all military units above the company level.[33] Party committees across the military participate in the planning work that informs the development of budgets for their respective units.[34] Financial departments at all levels of command in the theaters and services carry out the detailed budgetary work for military units from the national to the regimental levels. Theater- and service-level auditing offices oversee military spending activities for their military units.[35]

Table 2.1 differentiates among the key actors in the PLA's budgeting process.

---

[30] Lawrence and Lee, 2021.

[31] Blasko et al., 2006.

[32] LeighAnn Luce and Erin Richter, "Handling Logistics in a Reformed PLA: The Long March Toward Joint Logistics," in Philip C. Saunders, Arthur S. Ding, Andrew Scobell, Andrew N. D. Yang, and Joel Wuthnow, eds., *Chairman Xi Remakes the PLA: Assessing Chinese Military Reforms*, National Defense University Press, 2019.

[33] Kevin Pollpeter and Kenneth W. Allen, eds., *The PLA as Organization v.2.0*, China Aerospace Studies Institute, July 27, 2018, p. 41.

[34] Zhang Yunbi, "Reform Advisors Come into View," *China Daily*, August 2, 2016.

[35] State Council Information Office of the People's Republic of China, *China's National Defense*, December 11, 2006.

TABLE 2.1

Key Actors in the PLA's Budgeting Process

Actor	Description and Role
Politburo Standing Committee	Supreme decisionmaking body in China that consists of the seven most senior CCP members. The committee reviews and approves the annual state budget.
Politburo	The Political Bureau of the CCP is a key decisionmaking body comprising 24 senior leaders. It meets infrequently and is responsible for reviewing the annual state budget.
NPC	China's national legislature and the highest authority in the government bureaucracy. The NPC reviews the draft budget, approves the official budget, and reports on its implementation.
NPC Standing Committee	A select group of NPC delegates responsible for supervising and implementing the central and subnational budgets. The committee also reviews and approves proposed budgetary changes and approves the final accounts of the central government.
NPC Financial and Economic Affairs Committee	Reviews the preliminary proposals for the draft budget and the initial draft of the central government's final accounts.
State Council	The chief administrative authority of China's government; administers the work of central ministries and oversees the work of subnational governments. It consists of 35 senior government officials, including the premier, vice premier, and the heads of ministries.
MOF	This cabinet-level ministry of the State Council is responsible for macroeconomic policy and administering the annual budget.
MOF National Defense Department	Within the MOF, the National Defense Department is an internal agency responsible for all military-related budget work.
CMC	The highest-level military leadership organization, the CMC is traditionally chaired by the head of the CCP. It is responsible for military plans and overseeing the military's budget development and execution.
CMC Strategic Planning Department	Researches strategic issues and assists with planning; its work informs the PLA's budget.
CMC Logistics Support Department	Oversees the military's logistics and handles much of the staff work for the national military budget.
CMC Auditing Office	Provides oversight support for the PLA's budget execution.
CCP committees in the PLA	CCP committees consisting of key leaders and decisionmakers in the military theaters and services from the national to the regimental levels oversee the planning for their respective budgets.
PLA financial departments	The financial departments in the headquarters of military theaters and services from the national to the regimental levels carry out the detailed staff work for their respective budgets.
PLA auditing offices	Auditing offices located in the headquarters of military theaters and services from the national to regimental levels supervise the spending by their respective military units.

Planning and Programming

In China, the central party leadership is responsible for providing strategic direction for the country—not just in defense but also in all other policy areas. Central leaders develop strategic goals, which are published in NPC reports every five years. These reports contain assessments of key threats, national strategic goals, and general guiding principles on how to achieve those goals.[36] According to the strategy outlined in these reports, the central leadership oversees the development of five-year work plans. The general guidelines set the tone, objectives, and principles for all state policy work, including the military's work. By design, this central guidance tends to be vague, setting the tone with broad targets. This approach permits considerable flexibility and experimentation on the part of subordinate ministries and subnational governments.

Although China's five-year plans no longer serve the purpose of controlling and administering the entire economy's activities (as authorities attempted to do from 1949 to the late 1970s), the plans remain important instruments of government policy and finance. In recognition of the enormous complexity of China's economy, authorities have labeled these policy blueprints five-year *programs* [规划] to emphasize the difference between them and the often disastrous Maoist *plans* [计划].[37] The State Council, in turn, translates the guidelines into an outline that is approved by the NPC the following spring. Once the NPC approves the outline, provincial governments and ministries (led by their respective party committees and congresses) translate the outline into detailed annual and multiyear work plans and subplans; this is where much of the work occurs to translate plans into policies. The subplans provide measurable targets for policy implementation based on the conditions and resources of relevant government bodies. The subplans also set the parameters for policy strategies and enumerate performance evaluation indicators.[38] The central leadership reviews and approves the annual government budget plans and nationwide regulations on government finance and budgets.

The military follows a similar pattern. In accordance with the national development strategy put forward by CCP leadership in the NPC report and other key documents, senior political and military leaders develop a *national security strategy* [国家安全战略]. The CMC, in turn, develops a supporting military strategy, which is codified into a set of instructions known as *military strategic guidelines* [军事战略方针]. The military strategic guidelines designate the principal threats facing the country, goals for military modernization, and gen-

---

[36] Timothy R. Heath, *China's New Governing Party Paradigm: Political Renewal and the Pursuit of National Rejuvenation*, Routledge, 2014.

[37] Sebastian Heilmann and Oliver Melton, "The Reinvention of Development Planning in China, 1993–2012," *Modern China*, Vol. 39, No. 6, November 2013.

[38] Oliver Melton, "China's Five-Year Planning System: Implications for the Reform Agenda," testimony before the U.S.-China Economic and Security Review Commission, April 22, 2015.

eral principles on the use of military force.[39] From these guidelines, the CMC develops an evaluation of military strategic capabilities [军事战略能力评估]. Scholars Luo Jiancheng and Geng Kui define *military strategic capabilities* as the "total capability of the military to use resources to achieve strategic objectives," encompassing "the resources and capabilities to build, develop, and use military power" in peacetime and war.[40] They explain that the evaluation of military strategic capabilities involves three tasks:

1. recognizing the existing level of military capabilities
2. clarifying the gap between actual and desired capabilities
3. supporting the formulation of national strategic objectives.

Luo and Geng note that the last task involves advising national planners and decision-makers on the potential achievement of national strategic goals and informing the CMC's military strategic guidelines. From this evaluation of capabilities, the CMC develops a set of requirements [需求].[41]

Drawing on all these inputs, the CMC develops a variety of plans, the most important of which is the *Outline of the Five-Year Program for Military Development*. This document guides service and theater command planning. Led by their respective party committees, the services and commands develop annual and multiyear subplans that articulate work plans, goals, strategies, and measurable performance indicators. The *Outline of the Five-Year Program for Military Development* is not the military's only plan, however. In a reflection of the variety of plans approved by the central party leadership, the military leadership approves other types of long-term plans to serve the PLA's modernization needs. Examples include long-term plans to develop military talent and defense-related science and technology capabilities, which may have ten- to 15-year timelines.[42] The military plans and subplans are not available to the public.

However, China's 2019 defense white paper, *China's National Defense in the New Era*—which is considered an authoritative statement of the country's defense policy—notes that the PLA had adopted "demand-oriented planning" and that resource allocation had become "planning-led" as of 2019.[43] The PLA's adoption of demand-oriented planning and planning-

---

[39] Joel Wuthnow and M. Taylor Fravel, "China's Military Strategy for a 'New Era': Some Change, More Continuity, and Tantalizing Hints," *Journal of Strategic Studies*, March 8, 2022.

[40] Luo Jiancheng and Geng Kui, "Improve the Strategic Evaluation System and Improve the Quality and Efficiency of Military Building" ["完善战略评估体系提升军队建设质量效益"], *China Military Science* [中国军事科学], August 20, 2021.

[41] Luo and Geng, 2021.

[42] "Xi Focus: PLA Striving to Build World Class Military Under Xi's Leadership," Xinhua, August 2, 2022.

[43] State Council Information Office of the People's Republic of China, 2019, p. 28. *Demand-oriented planning* is the process of forecasting the demands for resource expenditure. A *planning-led allocation of resources* is one in which resources are provided according to the needs set by a plan.

led resource allocation likely happened between 2015 and 2019; the 2015 white paper titled *China's Military Strategy* lists those tasks as incomplete.[44] The 2019 white paper noted that plans and programs had been developed for the entire military, the services, the branches, and the People's Armed Police—and that the military had streamlined its procedures for evaluating, supervising, and managing its five-year programs.[45] These changes might have mitigated what some writings on military planning and budgeting had cited as long-standing problems, such as duplicative plans, weak coordination across departments, and inefficient implementation, in part owing to vague central guidance.[46]

Annual military budgets are formulated in accordance with the general goals set by the theater and service party congresses and committees in multiyear and annual work plans.[47] But the annual budgets are not derived exclusively from top-down planning requirements. The budgets are also informed by bottom-up requirements submitted by the financial departments of military units. These submissions detail the baseline spending needs and anticipated expenditures of the units. This approach is consistent with the 2014 Budget Law, which states that the previous year's budget, performance evaluation results of relevant expenditures, and forecasts of revenue and expenditures for the current year should all be taken into consideration when formulating the budget.[48]

As mentioned in the previous section, the CMC's GLD used to manage the military budget process. Nonetheless, the process appears to be nearly the same today. According to a 2007 presentation by PLA Major General Gong Xianfu, the process used to begin with units submitting their budget requirements up the chain of command starting in April. Draft budgets were completed in June and submitted to the military regional commands in August or September. The GLD was responsible for compiling the budgets and submitting them to the CMC for approval.[49] Meanwhile, the PLA received its budget ceiling in November, and the draft budget for the entire military was reviewed at the All Military Logistics Conference in November. Once the CMC approved the draft budget, it was passed to the MOF, which discussed the budget plan with the GLD, integrated it into the central budget draft, and sent the document to the State Council and NPC for formal approval. The GLD was then responsible

---

[44] State Council Information Office of the People's Republic of China, *China's Military Strategy*, May 27, 2015.

[45] State Council Information Office of the People's Republic of China, 2019.

[46] Fang Zhengqi, "Overall Planning Measures for Resources for Building Our Military Under New Conditions" ["新形势下我军建设资源统筹对策"], *Military Economic Research* [军事经济研究], November 2015.

[47] Gao Kai, "Strengthening Institutional Design to Improve Military Budget Execution" ["加强制度设计提高军事预算执行力"], *Military Economic Research* [军事经济研究], February 2011.

[48] Xin Zhiming, "Revised Budget Law to Have Far Reaching Effect," *China Daily*, September 11, 2014.

[49] Stephen S. Balut, Dennis C. Blair, Chester Arnold, John T. Hanley, Katy O. Hassig, Stanley A. Horowitz, David E. Hunter, Gong Xianfu, Jiang Shilang, Chen Yongxing, et al., *Proceedings of the Second IDA-CIISS Workshop: Common Security Challenges and Defense Personnel Costs*, Institute for Defense Analyses, January 2008, p. 86.

for implementing the budget from the top down to the relevant PLA units. Although the GLD was disbanded in the reforms of 2015 and replaced by 15 smaller departments directly under CMC control, the budget process likely takes a similar course today; the process described by Major General Gong in 2007 is similar to the process described in Chapter 4, "Budget Preparation," of the 2014 Budget Law.[50] The principal change is that the responsibilities formerly held by the GLD reside within the Logistics Support Department and the Strategic Planning Office in the CMC (Figure 2.3).[51]

As of this writing, the Logistics Support Department coordinates with relevant general departments to analyze, calculate, and verify the annual budget requests submitted by the services and military theater commands. The CMC reviews and approves the military budget, which the Logistics Support Department then submits to the National Defense Department within the MOF. The National Defense Department consults with the Logistics Support Department, refers to the state's medium- and long-term fiscal plans, and considers the estimated annual revenue before putting forward a military expenditure plan to be included in the central government's annual budget draft. Upon approval of the central government's draft budget by the State Council, both the NPC Standing Committee and the NPC Finance and Economic Committee review and approve the budget, which they forward to the full NPC for approval. Once the NPC approves the central government's budget, the MOF informs the Logistics Support Department of the approved defense budget in writing.

FIGURE 2.3
China's Annual Military Budget Cycle

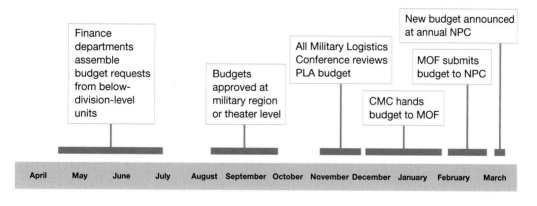

SOURCE: Features information from Blasko et al., 2006, p. 38.
NOTE: The figure shows the annual budget cycle as of 2006.

---

[50] "Budget Law of the People's Republic of China," 2014.

[51] For an overview of PLA reforms, see Philip C. Saunders, Arthur S. Ding, Andrew Scobell, Andrew N. D. Yang, and Joel Wuthnow, eds., *Chairman Xi Remakes the PLA: Assessing Chinese Military Reforms*, National Defense University Press, 2019.

The defense budget is then implemented from the top down within the PLA through pre-scribed procedures.[52]

Budgeting and Execution

In October 2014, the CMC implemented a military expenditure performance management system to assess the effectiveness of defense spending.[53] The system involves developing per-formance objectives for each military budget item, including technical and tactical indica-tors, expected results and benefits, cost and expense levels, and the degree of contribution to combat effectiveness. Each budget item's performance is closely monitored, and prompt measures are taken to rectify any deviations from the predetermined performance target. Military projects receive performance evaluations, which are then submitted for review and judgment.

Initially, the military's guidelines for expenditure performance management spanned five categories of projects for performance evaluation pilots at the headquarters and military region levels. The categories included training simulation equipment and hospital financial management. In 2020, the PLA fully rolled out these guideline-driven performance evalu-ations. Now, units are required to examine their performance indicators from the previous year when drafting their new budgets for the next year. In addition to the CMC system, the MOF evaluates military expenditure performance using such indicators as asset-liability ratio, profit rate, net present value, and net cash profit in accordance with Military Account-ing System regulations.[54]

Financial departments at the five theater joint commands and the services from the national to regimental levels are responsible for the appropriation, management, and super-vision of defense funds.[55]

Oversight

China's military finance system has undergone structural and regulatory changes in recent years to provide the CMC with greater oversight of budgeting, accounting, and auditing pro-cesses. In November 2014, authorities moved the central Audit Office out of the GLD and directly under the CMC to give the office greater independent operating power.[56] In addition

---

[52] Balut et al., 2008, p. 86.

[53] "The Central Military Commission Approves the Implementation of Military Expenditure Performance Management" ["中央军委批准推行军费绩效管理"], *Beijing News*, October 27, 2014.

[54] Zhang Yang, Sun Min, and Li Wenzhong, "Government Budget Performance Management and Implica-tions for Military Budget Management" ["政府预算绩效管理及对军队预算管理的启示"], *China Manage-ment Informationization*, Vol. 24, No. 18, September 2021.

[55] State Council Information Office of the People's Republic of China, 2006.

[56] "Xi Jinping Signs an Order: The PLA Audit Office Is Placed Under the Central Military Commission" ["习近平签署命令:解放军审计署划归中央军委建制"], Xinhua, November 6, 2014.

to auditing revenue, expenditures, and cost-effectiveness assessments, the Audit Office can carry out joint audits of military-civil fusion development projects.

In 2019, the Finance Bureau of the CMC's Logistics Support Department implemented "interim measures for the settlement and reimbursement of military unit expenses" to centralize the settlement and reimbursement process, address the proliferation of fake invoices and contracts, transfer expenses where needed, and appropriately reimburse personal expenses.[57] The Finance Bureau's responsibilities are divided between its business department and its financial department. The business department is responsible for collecting, sorting, and reviewing settlement and reimbursement vouchers, which requires going through approval procedures in accordance with regulations and authenticating the expenses. The financial department is responsible for reviewing settlement and reimbursement vouchers, reviewing reimbursement procedures, handling fund payments, overseeing the compliance of expenditures and procedures, and ensuring the integrity of payments. The sign-off leader is responsible for signing and approving expense settlements and reimbursements; the leader is also responsible for their authenticity.[58]

Analysis of China's Defense Budgeting Process

Strengths

China's military budgeting process has several strengths. First, it focuses investment on priority projects. Because political power is centralized, authorities can speedily direct funds to priority projects. The significant membership overlap between the CMC and the upper echelons of the CCP reduces the need for coordination for priority projects.

Second, China's system allows for generous and consistent funding of priority projects over long periods. The focus on long-term plans, such as the PLA's five-year programs and other plans, allows China's government to sustain funding over many years for projects deemed to be of high strategic value. The emphasis on planning and top-level direction ensures consistent funding for these projects; thus, China's programs are not prone to leaving priorities hanging or allowing interruptions in systems with a diversity of stakeholders.

A third potential advantage is the high level of coordination among government plans and budgets. This coordination can be seen across the intricate network of plans and subplans developed at all levels of the military, all of which inform relevant military budgets at the theater, service, and national levels.

---

[57] Sun Xingwei, Qui Mingjie, and Li Jian, "The Relevant Person in Charge of the CMC Logistic Support Department Finance Bureau Answered Reporters' Questions on the Latest Expense Settlement and Reimbursement Regulations" ["军委后勤保障部财务局有关负责人就最新经费结算报销规定问题答记者问"], *PLA Daily*, May 20, 2019.

[58] Sun, Qui, and Li, 2019.

Fourth, China has strengthened its mechanisms for evaluating and executing its military budgets, most importantly by centralizing logistics and finance functions within the CMC. This centralization can help China not only streamline these processes but also resist the formation of powerful interest groups, which has occurred in the past. The recent reforms could also allow the CMC to check corruption more effectively in logistics-related offices.

In sum, China's political system likely facilitates the rapid and generous allocation of resources to acquisition projects deemed to be of strategic importance. The centralized nature of the planning and budgeting processes allows the government to quickly marshal resources when needed. At the same time, China's system provides considerable flexibility for lower-level managers to adjust their acquisition and spending decisions.

Challenges

China's military budgeting process has several challenges. The first and most serious one is weak oversight and the potential for corruption, misuse of funds, and waste. China's budgeting processes are hampered by clientelism (bribery), patronage (favoritism), and other forms of corruption that pervade the defense industries. Powerful SOEs continue to operate in a highly inefficient and wasteful manner, partly because of the political power they exert. Articles and commentaries in military media acknowledge that problems related to military budget management, accounting, and financing are widespread—essentially mirroring critiques of China's overall budgeting processes. A 2016 *PLA Daily* article notes that problems of "soft constraints" on defense construction spending had "still not been solved."[59]

The separation of budget formulation from execution and supervision has reportedly produced additional waste and mismanagement. Specifically, this separation means that the financial departments that are responsible for executing policies are often not familiar with military needs on the ground; consequently, the financial departments allocate defense funds based on their ability to *supply* rather than on factual *demand*. A 2010 article in *Military Economic Research* notes that the separation of budget formulation from budget execution had resulted in "problems of exceeding the budget, not executing the budget, and changing the budget without authorization." The article characterizes these problems as "persistent" and as appearing in numerous units.[60] A 2017 assessment by military scholars published in *Review of Economic Research* suggests that the divide between budget formulation and execution remained an ongoing issue. Notably, the performance evaluation measures that were introduced by reforms have tended to focus on budgetary compliance and the proper distribution

---

[59] Han Guoxian [侯永波], "What Does Reform Bring National Defense Building?" ["改革给国防建设带来什么?"], *PLA Daily* [解放军报], January 25, 2016.

[60] Xu Mingzhi, "Diagnosis and Treatment of Weakened Enforcement on Military Budget" ["军队预算执行力弱化诊疗"], *Military Economic Research* [军事经济研究], November 2010.

of funds rather than on a budget item's effectiveness. This divide has sometimes led to an incomplete picture of the budget execution results and thus to misinformed budget plans.[61]

Second, the long-term focus of projects may constrain flexibility. It is possible that authorities struggle to adapt and modify requirements in a timely manner. Once the central leadership decides on a course and commits considerable resources to it, the government and military entities involved in its execution could develop clients and patronage networks that prove difficult to change, should new needs emerge. The 2017 article published in *Review of Economic Research* suggests that flexibility is also constrained in the policy implementation stage. Specifically, policy tasks are delegated based on entrenched "policy territories" of departmental leaders rather than on the changing needs of key projects, resulting in the misalignment of short-, medium-, and long-term plans and the fragmentation of funds.[62]

Some PLA sources at least partially blame both of these first two problems—weak oversight and inflexibility—on the power of party committees to dominate the financial departments of China's government agencies and ministries. One 2011 article states that, although the typical financial department is "nominally the formulator of military budgets," it acts "more as a department executing policies of the party committee" and therefore "lacks management and control powers."[63]

Third, a lack of political opposition could produce a military planning process that is devoid of any competition of ideas at the top level, leaving the leadership susceptible to overlooking important counterarguments in its planning. This lack of opposition could also make the process more vulnerable to manipulation by powerful SOEs and other vested interests that benefit from current budgeting processes at the expense of funding for truly innovative and strategic ideas.[64]

Fourth, a lack of budgeting expertise has compounded China's budgetary mismanagement problems.[65] In 2013, the PLA's Department of Finance introduced a new reform measure requiring expert review "for the formulation and execution of budgets by operational units of the general departments."[66] A major driver of this reform appears to have been the PLA's desire to incorporate more-accurate and more-standardized data into its budget decisions. In 2014, *PLA Daily* reported that the military would establish a "contingent of part-

---

[61] Wang Zhe, Zhang Xing, Qi Zhihong, and Wang Qingjuan, "Analysis on the Construction of the National Defense Medium-Term Budget Management System" ["国防预算中期管理制度的构建分析"], *Review of Economic Research* [经济研究参考], 2017.

[62] Wang et al., 2017.

[63] Huang Ruixin [黄瑞新], "On PLA Carrying Out the Performance Budget System" ["对我军实行绩效预算制度的思考"], *Military Economics Research* [军事经济研究], June 2011, pp. 5–6.

[64] Xu, 2010.

[65] Xu, 2010.

[66] "Budget of PLA Headquarters Focuses on Combat Power, Reducing Consumable Expenditures by 23%" ["解放军总部预算向战斗力聚焦 消耗性开支压减23%"], *China News*, June 18, 2013.

time statisticians with consumption data" to "provide reliable information sources and data support for the decisionmaking."[67]

Fifth, there appears to be a lack of quantifiable indicators in the large-scale planning of defense spending. Although Article 35 of China's National Defense Law stipulates that national defense spending should reflect national defense needs and national economic development, there are no procedural guidelines for quantifying defense demand and national supply. A 2013 article in the *Journal of PLA Nanjing Institute of Politics* laments that China needs to adopt a more sophisticated defense spending review process, similar to the U.S. Quadrennial Defense Review.[68] The lack of a comparative analysis by specialized agencies to determine the proper ratio of national defense spending to national financial capacity means that the ratio is often arbitrarily based on the preferences of leaders.

In sum, despite reforms, China's military budget process continues to suffer from problems related to weak oversight, mismanagement, insufficient expertise, and manipulation by vested interests.

Applicability

China's budget system reflects its historical experience with Soviet-style planning and budgets. Like its predecessors, China's system is well suited for allocating resources in a top-down, centralized manner to projects deemed to be of strategic importance. The centralized nature of the system, lack of independent oversight, and lack of independent analytic support mean that problems of corruption, inefficiency, and misuse of funds have long plagued China's military budget system. Beijing has sought to overcome the defects of the Soviet system by introducing greater flexibility into its planning process and adopting best practices to ensure that its budgets are more accountable, transparent, and efficient. Although a lack of publicly available data makes it difficult to evaluate with any confidence, the changes enacted by the 2014 Budget Law and military reorganization reforms could be helping modernize the budget process. However, there are reasons to be wary of overstating the potential improvements brought about by the recent reforms. Evaluations of the 2014 Budget Law on the broader political economy have generally bred pessimism, suggesting little progress in rectifying some of the larger systemic problems in government finance.[69] This may well be true for the PLA as well.

There may be some lessons for other countries that are seeking to improve and streamline their own processes. Establishing mechanisms that allow resources to be allocated on a

---

[67] Tao Shengxu Jinzhang, "PLA to Comprehensively Promote the Standardization of Business Funds" ["全军全面推进事业经费标准化建设"], *PLA Daily*, October 22, 2014.

[68] Li Zaiqian and Sun Zuo, "The Legal Regulation of China's National Defense Fund Allocation" ["论我国国防经费划拨的法律规制基于程序正当性的思考"], *Journal of PLA Nanjing Institute of Politics* [南京政治学学报], No. 3, 2013, pp. 100–104.

[69] Christine Wong, "Plus ça Change: Three Decades of Fiscal Policy and Central-Local Relations in China," *China: An International Journal*, Vol. 19, No. 4, November 2021.

timelier basis to strategically important projects could be crucial for ensuring timely resourcing of vital priorities. Likewise, developing plans that span several years could permit more-strategic and well-thought-out budgets to sustain longer-term projects.

Lessons from China's Defense Budgeting Process

There are at least four potential lessons for DoD from this review of China's defense budgeting process. See Table 2.2 for an overview of the lessons learned and potential actions for DoD.

Lesson 1: Flexibility Could Help Project Managers Serve Project Needs

One distinctive feature of China's process is the flexibility given to lower-level managers to make decisions and adjust spending and acquisitions to better serve project needs. Senior leaders provide general guidance and then delegate much of the actual planning and development work to lower-level managers. Data on how this arrangement has operated remain scarce in publicly available documents. We do not have access to information about how Chinese officials managed some of the most successful weapon developments, such as the hypersonics program.

However, insights could be inferred from details that are available about major initiatives, such as China's "two engines" project. Although hardly a resounding success, the management of the two engines project could be analogous to the management of China's successful development of hypersonic missiles because China's management of the hypersonic missiles project and other priority projects likely resembled the procedures followed in the two engines project. In 2013, the State Council launched a project to master aeroengines and industrial gas turbines, which shares many core technologies that could support military aircraft. In 2016, the project was given a budget of $15 billion. The State Council established the Two Engines Project Leading Small Group, which was composed of a small number of top government and industry leaders, to oversee the project. Housed within the Ministry of Industry and Information Technology, the Leading Small Group likely helps manage the budget and oversees relevant research and development, but further details of its activities remain scarce.[70]

Intriguingly, PLA researchers who have assessed the U.S. PPBE system's strengths and challenges have argued that its stringent processes lead to an inflexible approach to technological requirements, a misrepresentation of long-term defense strategy, and a misguided

---

[70] Peter Wood, Alden Wahlstrom, and Roger Cliff, *China's Aeroengine Industry*, China Aerospace Studies Institute, March 2020, p. 20.

deference to political influences.[71] DoD might wish to allow greater flexibility in its PPBE System so that portfolio managers can make changes quickly to stay in alignment with overall strategic guidance and plans as technologies and programs advance.

Lesson 2: Synchronized Plans and Budgets Could Offer Long-Term Benefits

China's approach features an elaborate system of planning in which lower-level military units, from the regiment level upward, develop plans and subplans that are designed to meet requirements assigned by higher-level plans, ultimately based on guidance from the CMC. China's system places a strong emphasis on top-down planning but allows some input from lower-level commands. This approach *does* have the drawback of dispersed planning, which could potentially lead to duplicative and wasteful efforts. However, the approach could also allow more-consistent and more-systematic budget planning.

DoD might want to consider methods to streamline procedures and processes to ensure a closer alignment of annual plans and budgets across the force with long-term strategies and resource plans.

Lesson 3: Performance Measurement Could Strengthen Expenditure Accountability

To overcome the pervasive issues of corruption, mismanagement of funds, and weak oversight, Chinese officials have adopted a series of regulations that align with strategic guidance in order to hold finance departments accountable for spending. Officials have required the use of a variety of indicators and measures to demonstrate the value of money spent and to control waste. The U.S. government has its own system of accounting and oversight, but DoD might consider modifying its performance metrics to ensure alignment not only with budgeted spending but also with the performance requirements of fielded platforms and weapon systems.

Lesson 4: Oversight Is Essential to Control Corruption and Ensure Proper Budget Execution

The most serious challenge in China's military and national budgeting processes is weak oversight and the potential for corruption, misuse of funds, and waste. There seems to be a trade-off between oversight and flexibility. A lesson for DoD may be the need to balance proper oversight with greater decentralization of authority to permit adaptive flexibility.

---

[71] Huai Fuli et al., 2015.

TABLE 2.2

Lessons from China's Defense Budgeting Process

Theme	Lesson Learned	Description
Decisionmakers and stakeholders	Lesson 1: Flexibility could help project managers serve project needs.	DoD could provide greater flexibility so portfolio managers could make changes to stay in alignment with guidance as technologies and programs advance.
Planning and programming	Lesson 2: Synchronized plans and budgets could offer long-term benefits.	DoD could add processes and procedures to strengthen the synchronization of annual, longer-term budgets and plans.
Budgeting and execution	Lesson 3: Performance measurement could strengthen expenditure accountability.	DoD could expand its set of measurement criteria to hold military expenditures accountable.
Oversight	Lesson 4: Oversight is essential to control corruption and ensure proper budget execution.	DoD might need to balance proper oversight with greater decentralization of authority to permit adaptive flexibility.

Conclusion

The military budget system of the PLA reflects China's broader approach to its finances and its political system. A highly centralized political system and a legacy of state industries and planning have meant that China's leaders excel at initiating and sustaining large-scale, expensive spending projects that they perceive to be strategically valuable. Moreover, the unavoidable need to delegate some authority to subnational actors has allowed authorities in China a degree of flexibility in spending implementation that has paid off considerably in some cases.

In the past two decades in particular, the PLA has made rapid progress in improving the technological sophistication and potential lethality of its forces. But it is difficult for U.S. policymakers to determine the extent to which that progress owes to China's ability to allocate and sustain funding for priority research endeavors. On one hand, the government's ability to ensure consistent funding for priority projects for years on end has likely contributed to its modernization successes. On the other hand, different factors have likely contributed as much or more to those successes. Decades of rapid growth have yielded vast resources, allowing the government to invest in building the infrastructure, research facilities, and skilled workforce that could help the country become a technological leader. Such investments have benefited the military and its aspirations to become more technologically advanced as well.[72]

Still, the advantages offered by China's budget system must be considered alongside its disadvantages. A lack of opposition, weak institutions, and the CCP's unchecked power have resulted in pervasive problems of weak accountability, corruption, and inefficiency.

Yet all things considered, our limited access to information on China's defense *budgeting* successes and failures means that we need to look beyond what we could determine from our

---

[72] Weinbaum et al., 2022.

case study's focus on general PPBE practices and toward specific instances of China's weapon *development* successes and failures. For instance, a good illustration of how factors beyond budgeting have contributed to China's modernization successes can be seen in the case of hypersonic missiles. In March 2023, U.S. intelligence officials reported that China might have already deployed a hypersonic missile capable of striking U.S. military bases in the Pacific. The officials noted that China leads the United States in this particular technology; the U.S. military has not yet deployed such a weapon.[73] China's hypersonic missile success builds on a robust and world-leading missile program. For decades, China has developed the technologies, personnel, and industrial infrastructure required to produce vast quantities of ballistic missiles, while the United States has limited its development and production of similar weapons owing to its adherence to arms control treaties.[74]

Conversely, the limitations of the military's budget program in driving PLA modernization can be seen in instances in which top-priority projects, despite generous and sustained funding, have failed to achieve modernization goals. Since the 1990s, for example, China has designated the development and manufacture of cutting-edge jet engines a national priority and committed billions of dollars accordingly. Yet the prioritization and sustained funding permitted by the country's centralized budget process have failed to overcome challenges in China's defense industrial capacity and technical expertise, resulting in a still-underperforming engine sector.[75] Similarly, authorities have designated the development of advanced semiconductors a national priority; yet despite having spent well more than $100 billion, China has failed to achieve breakthroughs in this area—much of the money was lost to fraud, corruption, and misallocation.[76]

Limitations in China's defense industry compound—and perhaps mirror—many of the challenges in China's budget process. SOEs manufacture all of China's domestically produced weapons and platforms. Years of rapidly growing defense budgets have led to an enormous expansion in the revenues of the defense SOEs.[77] However, because the firms lack a profit incentive, they generally suffer from severe problems of inefficiency, waste, and bloat. Moreover, the defense SOEs, like other major SOEs, have accrued sufficient wealth and power that they can resist efforts to control their operations. Chinese leaders have attempted to improve

---

[73] Jeff Seldin, "US Defense Officials: China Is Leading in Hypersonic Weapons," *Voice of America*, March 10, 2023.

[74] Paul Bernstein and Dain Hancock, "China's Hypersonic Weapons," *Georgetown Journal of International Affairs*, January 27, 2021.

[75] Benjamin Brimelow, "China Is Trying to Fix the Engine Problem Plaguing Its Fighter Jets," *Business Insider*, June 6, 2021.

[76] Elliot Ji, "Great Leap Nowhere: The Challenges of China's Semiconductor Industry," *War on the Rocks*, February 23, 2023.

[77] Fenella McGerty and Meia Nouwens, "China's Military Modernization Spurs Growth for State-Owned Enterprises," *Defense News*, August 8, 2022.

the market competitiveness of SOEs for years but have not succeeded. Chinese SOEs remain less profitable and less efficient than firms in which the state does not have ownership.[78]

Although China forbids political actors from injecting themselves into the budget process in the way that Congress and U.S. military services can in the United States, Beijing faces its own problems of weak oversight and political lobbying for defense spending, along with their consequences. Because the general secretary depends on the support of the PLA to remain in power, leaders since at least Jiang Zemin have often provided the PLA generous resources with little oversight. Under Jiang Zemin, the PLA gained a reputation for corruption and criminality through such activities as smuggling, prostitution, and bribery.[79] Authorities eventually cracked down, but Hu Jintao's reluctance to involve himself in overseeing the military spurred rampant corruption.[80] Xi Jinping's crackdown on corruption appears to have curbed the problem, at least to some extent, but like his predecessors, Xi has provided generous defense budgets partly to curry favor with military leaders and to ensure their loyalty. The PLA has accordingly been able to develop big-budget weapon programs with little civilian oversight, sometimes resulting in expensive acquisitions of dubious military value, such as its enormously costly aircraft carrier program.[81]

In short, the reforms initiated in recent years to improve the PLA's budget process have attempted to mitigate some of its long-standing problems. But the impact of these budgetary reforms on the military's modernization will likely pale next to more fundamental drivers of technological success or failure, such as the maturity of related industries and the availability of a workforce skilled in relevant technologies.

For the United States, the applicability of the lessons from the China case study will also invariably be constrained by the differences in the two countries' political systems. DoD likely will not find any simple way of replicating China's strengths through imitation, given the starkly different governmental systems of the United States and China. But finding analogous measures to achieve similar effects could be worthwhile. In particular, finding ways to ensure sustained, consistent funding for priority projects over many years or delegating more authority and granting greater flexibility to project and program managers could have beneficial effects on DoD budgeting practices. Given the intensity and likely endurance of U.S.-China competition, such innovations seem well worth exploring.

---

[78] Emilia M. Jurzyk and Cian Ruane, "Resource Misallocation Among Listed Firms in China: The Evolving Role of State-Owned Enterprises," International Monetary Fund Working Paper No. 2021/075, March 12, 2021.

[79] Andrew Scobell, *Chinese Army Building in the Era of Jiang Zemin*, Strategic Studies Institute, U.S. Army War College, July 2000.

[80] John Garnaut, "Rotting from Within: Investigating the Massive Corruption of the Chinese Military," *Foreign Policy*, April 16, 2012.

[81] Sam Roggeveen, "China's New Aircraft Carrier Is Already Obsolete: But It's Still a Powerful Signal of Beijing's Ambitions in a Post-U.S. Asia," *Foreign Policy*, April 25, 2018.

CHAPTER 3

Russia

Dara Massicot and Mark Stalczynski

Russia is 30 years past a painful transition from a Soviet planned economy to a market economy. Although it has largely left its Soviet planning model in the past, it has carried forward certain ideas and legacies. For example, in Russia, competition between defense firms is not viewed as an inherently good thing that could spur innovation and increase productivity. Instead, it is viewed as a mechanism that dilutes available funds. State ownership is viewed as a source of protection from international markets and sanctions and as a mechanism to keep unproductive companies afloat.

Russia does not have a formal name (like PPBE) for its budgeting and programming processes, and its defense budgeting process is different from that of the United States.[1] Russia can be fiscally conservative at the federal level, avoiding deficits and engaging in little foreign borrowing, and its defense acquisition plans are often closely tied to military strategy and defense needs. However, opacity in multiple parts of Russia's PPBE-like process—compounded by insufficient oversight—often perpetuates corruption and generates outputs of varying quality from the defense industry. Russian leaders realize that their defense budget is limited and that they are outspent by their rivals; they speak often about their desire for a modern, capable military.[2] Although there have been attempts to reduce systemic graft and corruption in the past decade, the war in Ukraine has revealed these efforts to be insufficient.[3] Nevertheless, the desire for a well-oiled defense industrial base often collides with the excessive concentration of power in the executive branch and the informal practices that make business possible in modern Russia.

Our analysis found that Russia's planning, programming, and budgeting processes are built on fairly sound principles that were borrowed from Western countries in the 1990s in

---

[1] We describe several relevant aspects of Russia's process later in this chapter. However, it is worth mentioning that one important part of the programming side of Russia's PPBE-like process is the State Armaments Program (SAP), a planning and acquisition program with an implementation timeline of seven to ten years.

[2] "NATO's Military Spending Exceeds Russian Army Budget by 20 Times, Says Security Chief," 2021.

[3] Anderson, 2016; "The Military Prosecutor Called Theft in the Ministry of Defense 'Cosmic'" ["Военный прокурор назвал воровство в Минобороны «космическим»"], 2012.

the immediate post-Soviet economic transition.[4] Russia was required to make other budgetary reforms to receive loans from international organizations, such as the International Monetary Fund (IMF).[5] However, most of the PPBE-related problems Russia faces are in the *execution* phase, with key stakeholders often kept out of important decisions. This lack of transparency and lack of room for dissent allow mistakes to compound and graft to flourish. Oversight institutions are empowered in principle but not in practice.[6] Russia's defense industrial base can produce rugged and affordable products; however, institutional and structural factors cause it to underperform, lose large sums to cronyism and graft, and produce outputs of varying quality for the armed services.[7] Whereas Russia's system can be flexible and pivot to address different priorities when the Kremlin so demands—and without suffering much in the way of political or legal ramifications for canceling programs—the system does not allow sufficient oversight to ensure that it works effectively or produces uniformly high-quality products.

Russia's Defense Industrial Base: A Primer

Russia's defense industrial base comprises approximately 800 companies or entities with a workforce of nearly 3 million, consolidated under partial or majority state ownership.[8] Russia consolidated most of its defense firms under state control after 2007 to protect them on the global market, create efficiencies in Russia, and ensure more-direct oversight to account for funds and reduce graft. Consolidation began under the federal program known as Reform and Development of the Defense Industrial Complex, 2002–2006, which was motivated by a desire to vertically integrate various design, development, and manufacturing entities with a focus on distinct domains, in contrast to Soviet-era organizational structures.[9] The majority of Russia's defense sector is owned by the state corporation Rostec, which was established in

---

[4] Russia subject-matter expert, interview with the authors, November 2022.

[5] John Odling-Smee, "The IMF and Russia in the 1990s," International Monetary Fund Working Paper No. 04/155, August 2004.

[6] Julian Cooper, "The Russian Budgetary Process and Defence: Finding the 'Golden Mean,'" *Post-Communist Economies*, Vol. 29, No. 4, 2017.

[7] Andrew S. Bowen, *Russian Arms Sales and Defense Industry*, Congressional Research Service, R46937, October 14, 2021. The Pentagon briefed the media in March 2022 that Russian precision-guided munitions had a failure rate of between 20 and 60 percent, which was described as a result of fusing and accuracy problems, along with a failure to explode upon arriving at their targets (Schneider, 2022).

[8] Janes, 2022b.

[9] Janes, 2022b. Under the Soviet model, production of systems was purposefully dispersed across Russia to preserve capabilities in the event of war, while the reforms were meant to focus production at entities with the strongest potential for further development in their domain in a market economy (Cooper, 1993).

2007 by federal law.[10] The corporation is led by Sergey Chemezov, a close associate of Russia's President Vladimir Putin.[11]

Defense companies across sectors are grouped under various holding companies, which are directly subordinate to Rostec. These holding companies include Almaz-Antey (air defense), United Aircraft Corporation (aircraft), Tactical Missiles Corporation (precision-guided missiles), Radio-Electronic Technologies (electronic warfare), and United Shipbuilding Corporation (naval vessels). Some major holdings are controlled by the Federal Agency for State Property Management, including Almaz-Antey, which oversees approximately 50 entities that produce ground- and sea-based air defenses, and United Shipbuilding Corporation, which oversees approximately 40 entities that are responsible for 80 percent of commercial and naval shipbuilding in Russia.[12] The majority of defense industrial base entities are state-owned and/or state-controlled through Rostec; the state's shares are managed by the Ministry of Trade and Development. However, there are defense industrial entities with partial private ownership, such as Kalashnikov (~75-percent private), Kamaz (~50-percent private), and Russian Helicopters (~12-percent private).[13] In Table 3.1, we list 18 significant entities under the control of Rostec.

Although consolidating firms under state control has generated efficiencies, consolidation and protectionist policies have also stymied innovation, given the lack of domestic competition. Furthermore, corruption has long plagued Russia's defense industry and its government more broadly. In 2012, Russian and Western analysts estimated that 20–40 percent of annual funding from the SDO for military procurement was lost because of corruption, inflated prices for military goods, or the use of earmarked allocations for other purposes.[14] These findings led to various reforms: imposing larger fines and criminal penalties on individuals and organizations, moving responsibility for the SDO to Russia's MoD, and paying defense industry entities via restricted accounts at state-owned banks.[15]

However, as evidenced by the 2022 war in Ukraine, corruption persists in Russia's defense industrial base. Official accounts from the United States and unofficial reports from Ukrainian and Russian social media have revealed a Russian Army that lacks appropriate equipment, logistics, and even first-aid kits.[16] Additionally, observers have documented Russian

---

[10] Federal Law of the Russian Federation No. 270-FZ, On the State Corporation for the Promotion of the Development, Manufacture, and Export of High-Tech Products ("Rostec"), November 23, 2007.

[11] Janes, "State Corporation Rostec," *Janes World Defence Industry*, September 7, 2022a.

[12] Janes, 2022b.

[13] Janes, 2022b.

[14] Anderson, 2016; "The Military Prosecutor Called Theft in the Ministry of Defense 'Cosmic'" ["Военный прокурор назвал воровство в Минобороны «космическим»"], 2012. The SDO is known as the *Gosudarstvennyy oborony zakaz*, or GOZ, in Russian.

[15] Anderson, 2016.

[16] Beliakova, 2022; Cranny-Evans and Ivshina, 2022; Lee, 2022; Schneider, 2022.

TABLE 3.1

Major Russian Defense Firms Controlled by Rostec

Company	Domain	Description of Products
Avtomatika	Electronics	Advanced precision weapons
High Precision Systems	Precision weapons	Advanced precision weapons
Kalashnikov	Other	Small arms
Kamaz	Army	Heavy commercial and military vehicles
Kurganmashzavod	Army	Infantry fighting vehicles
Lipetsk Caterpillar Tractor Plant	Army	Treads for air defense systems
Radio-Electronic Technologies	Electronics	Electronic warfare systems (~75 entities)
Rosoboronexport	Other	State defense export organization
Ruselectronics	Electronics	Communications, radar, security, and robotic systems
Russian Helicopters	Aerospace	Helicopters
Shvabe	Electronics	Electro-optical systems (~65 entities)
Specchemistry	Precision weapons	Components for missiles and ammunition
TechMash	Precision weapons	Ammunition for artillery and grenade launchers
Technodinamika	Aerospace	Military and civilian aircraft components
United Aircraft Corporation	Aerospace	Aircraft
United Engine Corporation	Aerospace	Aircraft propulsion
Uralvagonzavod	Ground	Armored fighting vehicles and tanks (~20 entities)
Volgograd Machine Building Plant	Ground	Infantry fighting vehicles

SOURCES: Features information from Janes, 2022a; Janes, 2022b.

equipment without its necessary defensive components, including missing or hollowed-out explosive reactive armor on T-80 battle tanks.[17] Transparency International, a nonprofit research, monitoring, and advocacy organization, attributes the high incidence of corruption in Russia's defense industrial base to a lack of external, transparent oversight over functions analogous to PPBE—specifically, the functions of defense policy, budgeting, and acquisition.[18]

---

[17] Shinkman, 2022.

[18] Transparency International Defence and Security, June 2019–May 2020.

Overview of Russia's Defense Budgeting Process

Following the collapse of the Soviet Union, the Russian Federation had to transition its budgeting process to one based on free-market principles. In 1998, Russia adopted its Budget Code as part of this modernization effort. The Budget Code lists the budget's chapters (e.g., Chapter 1 is Revenues, Chapter 2 is Expenditures, Chapter 2.1 is General Government, Chapter 2.2 is National Defense) and designates budgetary roles for federal ministries and regional governments. It also sets the schedule for budget drafting and implementation, and it governs the handling of public debt and cash holdings by the Treasury.[19]

The Budget Code has been modified several times, such as in 2003 and 2004 to establish sovereign wealth funds and fiscal rules governing the use of diverted oil and gas revenues. The most significant change was in 2007, when Russia moved to three-year budgets, which is in line with recommendations and best practices from the IMF and the Organisation for Economic Co-operation and Development (OECD).[20] Three-year budgets—which are considered a medium-term expenditure framework—allow better planning and procurement based on reasonable economic forecasts while leaving some flexibility for reforms, political initiatives, or a rebalancing of expenditures across agencies. Three-year budgets also make budgeting a continuous exercise. The two planning years, or out-years, rely on conditionally appropriated baseline funding that is later adjusted for inflation, demographics, or other policy changes. Additionally, a share of forecasted expenditures for each out-year is set aside as a conditionally approved expenditure not assigned to a specific priority in a new budget year.[21] The 2020 budget, for example, conditionally appropriated unassigned funds of 516 billion rubles (2.5 percent of expenditures) and 1.1 trillion rubles (4.9 percent of expenditures) for 2021 and 2022, respectively.[22] Reallocation can—and often does—occur across different chapters of the budget, as long as it remains within the forecasted ceiling for expenditures; otherwise, additional revenues would have to be raised.[23] Unused budget allocations are transferred back to the budget within two days prior to the close of the fiscal year.[24]

The Russian Federation's fiscal years correspond to calendar years (January 1–December 31). The five phases of the budget process are *drafting* (March 1–October 1), *approval* (October 1–December 31), *implementation* (January 1–December 31), *reporting* (January 1–October 1), and *auditing* (January 1–September 1). Therefore, in a given year, implementation

---

[19] Budget Code of the Russian Federation, No. 145-FZ, July 31, 1998, effective January 1, 2023.

[20] Dirk-Jan Kraan, Daniel Bergvall, Ian Hawkesworth, Valentina Kostyleva, and Matthias Witt, "Budgeting in Russia," *OECD Journal on Budgeting*, Vol. 8, No. 2, 2008.

[21] Kraan et al., 2008.

[22] Russian Ministry of Finance, *Budget for Citizens to the Federal Law on the Federal Budget for 2020 and for the Planning Period of 2021 and 2022* [Бюджет Для Граждан к Федеральному закону о федеральном бюджете на 2020 год и на плановый период 2021 и 2022 годов], 2019.

[23] Kraan et al., 2008.

[24] Budget Code of the Russian Federation, 1998, effective January 1, 2023, Article 242.4.

of the current year's budget overlaps with reporting and auditing of the previous year's budget and drafting and approval of the following year's budget.[25] For an illustration of the annual budget process in Russia, see Figure 3.1.

The Ministry of Finance sends the draft budget, which draws on macroeconomic and socioeconomic forecasts from the Ministry of Economic Development, to the Duma (the lower house of Russia's legislature) and the President of Russia by October 1 of each year. Within three days, it is sent to various Duma committees for clarifications or corrections. It is also sent to the Federation Council (the upper house of the legislature) and the Accounts Chamber, which is the independent government entity responsible for financial control and auditing budget funds. The first reading of the draft budget by the Duma includes an assessment of the budget as a whole: socioeconomic forecasts (e.g., GDP, demographics, inflation), taxes, tariffs, expected revenues, expenditures, and debt service. The second reading focuses on appropriations, a review of the SDO, subsidies to regional and municipal governments, and future borrowing. The third reading is a vote by the Duma to pass the budget. Within five days of its passage, the budget is sent to the Federation Council, which then has 14 days

FIGURE 3.1
Annual Budget Process in Russia

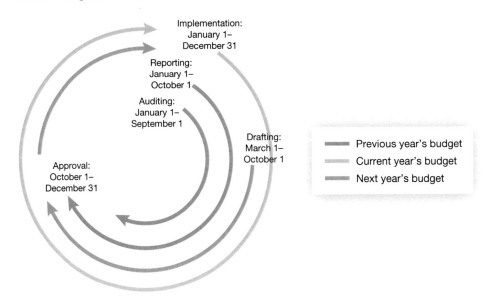

SOURCE: Features information from Budget.gov.ru, undated-a.

---

[25] Budget.gov.ru, "The Budget Process" ["Бюджетный Процесс"], webpage, undated-a.

to formally approve the budget. (The Federation Council does not undertake formal deliberations.) The budget is then sent to the President of Russia to be signed into law.[26]

Because total defense spending in Russia spans several of the federal budget's chapters, it is larger than what is presented in the National Defense chapter alone. Although the National Defense chapter specifies the primary appropriations for personnel, operations, and procurement for the Ministry of Defense and the Armed Forces of the Russian Federation, it does not include certain expenditures that member countries of the North Atlantic Treaty Organization define as *defense spending*, such as the Russian National Guard (which is addressed in the National Security and Law Enforcement chapter of the federal budget) or military pensions and military education (addressed in the Social Policy and Education chapters, respectively).[27] SIPRI estimated Russia's defense spending across all military-related components and reported that this spending amounted to $63.5 billion (roughly 4.8 trillion rubles) in 2021, or 4.1 percent of Russia's GDP (see Figure 3.2).[28]

In contrast with SIPRI's finding, Russia's budget appropriation in the National Defense chapter for 2021 was just 3.6 trillion rubles, or $48.5 billion.[29] The National Defense chapter contains appropriations for the Ministry of Defense—specifically, for the Russian Armed Forces, Modernization of the Armed Forces, Mobilization and Pre-Conscription Training, Mobilization of the Economy, Participation in Collective Peacekeeping Agreements, Nuclear Weapons Complex, International Military-Technical Cooperation, Research and Development, and a category designated for Other Expenditures. In recent years, more than 70 percent of National Defense chapter spending has been for the Russian Armed Forces. The portion of national defense spending that is classified increased from about 65 percent in 2021 and 2022 to 73 percent in 2023, following Russia's invasion of Ukraine. Approximately 15–16 percent of Russia's overall budget was classified in 2021 and 2022, whereas an estimated 23 percent was classified in the 2023 budget.[30]

---

[26] State Duma of the Federal Assembly of the Russian Federation, "How Is the Federal Budget Approved?" ["Как принимается федеральный бюджет"], September 30, 2021.

[27] The budget under the category of National Security and Law Enforcement was 4.4 trillion rubles in 2023, or approximately U.S. $72 billion at current exchange rates. Even more—4.9 trillion rubles, or approximately U.S. $80 billion—was budgeted for National Defense. National Security and Law Enforcement includes funding for the security services, law enforcement agencies (including border patrol and customs), the judicial system, and the Russian National Guard (Russian Ministry of Finance, 2019).

[28] SIPRI, undated, data as of October 31, 2022; Siemon T. Wezeman, "Russia's Military Spending: Frequently Asked Questions," Stockholm International Peace Research Institute, April 27, 2020.

[29] The figure was calculated using the ruble's average annual exchange rate calculated from the Central Bank of Russia's basic derived indicators of the ruble's exchange rate dynamics.

[30] Denis Dmitriev, "The Government Has Classified a Quarter of All Russian Spending for 2023 (This Is a Record). We Do Not Know What Six and a Half Trillion Rubles Will Be Spent on—but It Is Probably the War and Annexations" ["Правительство засекретило четверть всех расходов России на 2023 год (это рекорд) Мы не знаем, на что потратят шесть с половиной триллионов рублей—но, вероятно, это война и аннексия"], Meduza Project, October 12, 2022.

FIGURE 3.2

Russia's Total Defense Spending and Share of GDP

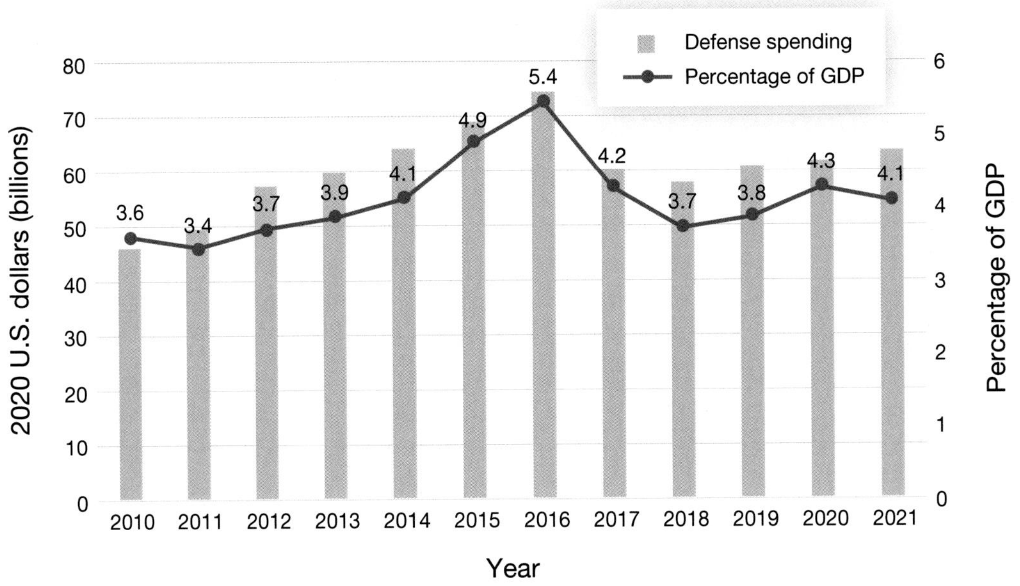

SOURCE: Features information from SIPRI, undated, data as of October 31, 2022.
NOTE: The total defense spending amounts are adjusted for inflation.

According to previous RAND analysis of publicly available information, classified components of the National Defense chapter budget for the Russian Armed Forces and for research and development support activities funded by the SDO. The SDO is the annual appropriation for military procurement to meet the SAP, the current ten-year procurement plan.[31] The SDO budget was estimated at 1.7 trillion rubles in 2020, or approximately $23 billion in nominal terms—nearly half of Russia's total national defense appropriation of 3.6 trillion rubles ($48.5 billion) for 2021, the following year.

However, our interviews with subject-matter experts and their analysis based on reporting and leaks to the media suggest that the actual SDO may be even larger and may be funded through other classified sections of Russia's national budget.[32] Although $23 billion for pro-

---

[31] Andrew Radin, Lynn E. Davis, Edward Geist, Eugeniu Han, Dara Massicot, Matthew Povlock, Clint Reach, Scott Boston, Samuel Charap, William Mackenzie, Katya Migacheva, Trevor Johnston, and Austin Long, *The Future of the Russian Military: Russia's Ground Combat Capabilities and Implications for U.S.-Russia Competition*, RAND Corporation, RR-3099-A, 2019, pp. 30–34. The SAP is known as *Gosudarstvennaia Programma Vooruzheniia*, or GPV, in Russian.

[32] Russia subject-matter expert, interview with the authors, November 2022; subject-matter interpretation of budget numbers in Aleksander Vorobyev, "Defense Companies Are Unable to Service Loans" ["оборонные предприятия не справлются с обслуживанием кредитов"], *Vedomosti*, October 17, 2019.

curement might seem modest in comparison with the U.S. procurement budget, we should note that military goods and services cost less in Russia because of several factors (e.g., wages, material inputs, PPP); therefore, Russia's government has a higher level of purchasing power within its borders.[33] Figure 3.3 presents the assumed SDO as a share of the National Defense chapter budget from 2012 to 2020. In the latter years of that period, the SDO share was about 50 percent of the total expenditures apportioned in the National Defense chapter of the budget. The increase in 2016 to 71 percent was because of large SDO payments to reduce the debt of defense industry firms, and direct support to the defense industry leveled off through 2020.[34]

There have been five SAP procurement plans since the dissolution of the Soviet Union. In the late 1990s, plans to improve procurement practices and modernize the Russian Armed Forces were dashed because of the harsh economic reality in the country. However, the legacy of the Soviet defense industrial base persists in Russia, and despite labor pool challenges and aging infrastructure, the country has maintained its status as a major arms exporter.[35] As stated previously, in 2007, the defense industrial base was consolidated under state-majority

FIGURE 3.3
State Defense Order as a Share of Russia's National Defense Budget

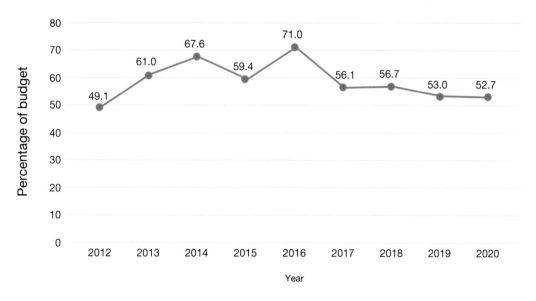

SOURCE: Features information from the Russian Treasury, *Reports on the Implementation of the Federal Budget* [Отчеты об исполнении федерального бюджета], 2012–2021, accessed October 31, 2022. Calculations were done by the authors using methodology outlined in Cooper, 2013, and Cooper, 2017.

---

[33] Wezeman, 2020.

[34] Radin et al., 2019.

[35] SIPRI, "Top List Trend-Indicator Value (TIV) of Arms Imports or Exports for a Selection of the Largest Suppliers or Recipients, Along with the TIV of Global Arms Imports or Exports," dataset, October 31, 2022.

ownership, and in 2009, with growing revenues from energy exports, Russia began a major military modernization push for its Army, Air Force, and Navy. Although the SAP is classified, details regularly surface in public statements made by Russia's President and high-ranking military officials. Table 3.2 provides an overview of all the SAPs since the founding of the Russian Federation with details about their funding and procurement goals.

Decisionmakers and Stakeholders

Budget decisionmakers and stakeholders in Russia are a combination of politicians, political appointees, and career civil servants. The Ministry of Finance prepares the draft budget—which includes the defense budget—with macroeconomic and socioeconomic forecasts from the Ministry of Economic Development. Both ministries are headed by political appointees confirmed by Russia's President, and the budget is prepared by career civil servants. The budget is then submitted to the Federal Assembly (legislature); it is debated in the Duma (lower house) and is then sent to the Federation Council (upper house) for a simple ceremonial passing, after which it is signed into law by the President of Russia. Other key decisionmakers and stakeholders in the budget process are the Treasury, the Accounts Chamber (which is responsible for auditing), and the Russian Central Bank (which holds the state's reserves),

TABLE 3.2

History of Russia's State Armaments Programs

SAP	Year Adopted	Approximate Funding Target (U.S. dollars)	Notes
SAP-2005	1996	Unavailable	Procurement goals were not met because of the difficult economic situation in the 1990s.
SAP-2010	2001	$80 billion	Procurement goals were tempered by inflation.
SAP-2015	2006	$80 billion	Procurement goals were not entirely fulfilled, but improvements were made in procurement planning.
SAP-2020	2011	$270 billion	Procurement goals of 70-percent modernized equipment were partially met, with major improvements to air defenses and aircraft and a shift to serial equipment production.
SAP-2027	2018	$270 billion	Procurement goals relate to military equipment, modernization (nuclear triad), research and development, storage infrastructure, more funding to ground forces, and the closure of gaps in aerospace forces.[a]

SOURCES: Features information from Radin et al., 2019; Richard Connolly and Mathieu Boulégue, *Russia's New State Armament Programme: Implications for the Russian Armed Forces and Military Capabilities to 2027*, Chatham House, May 2018.

NOTE: Dollar amounts are in nominal terms.

[a] The war in Ukraine will undoubtedly affect these goals, given Russia's losses.

all of which are headed by political appointees and run by civil servants.[36] Throughout the budget's implementation, the Treasury disperses funds to ministries and agencies based on its own reporting of cash needs as culled from the monthly, quarterly, and annual reports submitted by those ministries and agencies.[37]

Budget development is centralized, especially when it comes to defense spending. Minister of Defense Sergei Shoigu, Minister of Internal Affairs (which houses the National Guard) Vladimir Kolokoltsev, Director of the Federal Security Service Aleksander Bortnikov, and Director of the Foreign Intelligence Service Sergei Naryshkin all have permanent seats on the President's Security Council. These ministries and agencies are often referred to as the *power agencies*, unlike the Minister of Finance (Anton Siluanov), which is a nonpermanent member of the Security Council. As discussed later, the Security Council has great influence in long-term defense spending and procurement planning.

The extent to which the National Defense chapter of the budget has been revised before its passage in the past 20 years also suggests that legislators (Duma) have less influence over final defense spending than the President and the Security Council. As discussed previously, certain Soviet legacies continue in the defense industrial base. Such legacies include defense industrial cities created during the Soviet era, the economies of which are almost solely based on a defense manufacturer, not unlike some U.S. cities or towns that primarily serve a military base or installation. In Russia, examples include the town of Nizny Tagil, where the Uralvagonzavod tank factory is located; Naberzhnye Chelny, where the Kamaz truck manufacturing company is located; or the closed city of Sarov, home to the Russian Federal Nuclear Center and akin to Los Alamos, New Mexico. In past years, when the Ministry of Finance had to make substantial changes to the SDO because of a downturn or recession, it also had to be cognizant of changes that would negatively affect such defense industrial towns. In Russia, protection of these defense industrial cities has occurred at the ministerial and presidential levels; local Duma representatives and governors are neither independent nor particularly powerful political actors. Governors are appointed by the President, and the majority of the Duma's representatives hail from the United Russia political party (President Putin's party). Thus, major changes to protect such defense industrial cities and manufacturers were likely not the result of individual legislators acting on behalf of their constituencies (as in the U.S. House of Representatives and Senate) or out of fiscal prudence, but rather were the result of larger federal concerns about stability and preserving production lines.[38]

Russia's Military-Industrial Commission (*Voeynno Promyshlennaya Komissiya*, or VPK) shares the same name as its Soviet predecessor and plays a role in decisions related to funding the defense industry. It was reestablished, along with the federal Reform and Development of the Defense Industrial Complex, 2002–2006 program, to streamline funds, reduce misman-

---

[36] Budget.gov.ru, "Participants in the Budget Process" ["Участники бюджетного процесса"], webpage, undated-b.

[37] Kraan et al., 2008.

[38] Cooper, 2017.

agement in the defense industry, and potentially cope with Western sanctions.[39] The VPK works with the President and his Security Council, the Ministry of Finance, the Ministry of Economic Development, the Accounts Chamber, and members of the Duma to establish budget funding for the defense industry through the SDO. Interviews with subject-matter experts suggest that the VPK is not as powerful as it was during the Soviet era because most of the defense industry's power today is channeled through the state-owned defense conglomerate Rostec (which has a seat on the VPK). One key facet of Rostec's power may be the personal relationship between President Putin and Rostec executive director Sergey Chemezov. Beyond Rostec, other quasistate and quasimilitary entities (such as Rosatom, which handles nuclear munitions) work with the VPK and various budget stakeholders to ensure their own funding.[40]

The MoD, like all other ministries, must work within the Ministry of Finance framework to secure annual funding for its personnel and operations. Accordingly, the MoD has a deputy minister for financial and economic matters, and the Ministry of Finance has a designated department of budgetary policy for military services and the SDO.[41] Although the MoD must work within the realities of the budget for personnel and operations, the President wields heavy influence in developing the SDO, meeting early in the process with the Security Council, the Ministry of Finance, the VPK, and other members of the presidential administration to set defense funding priorities.[42] Furthermore, during legislative review of the draft budget, the Security Council can function as a means for the MoD to argue against funding reductions deemed detrimental to national security.[43]

Planning and Programming

The SAP is Russia's main document for defense planning and programming, and it is funded annually through the SDO. This is a top-down approach to planning and programming. Existing methods for determining the Russian Armed Forces' requirements were largely inherited from the Soviet Union, and Russia may not have a methodology for determining the resources or costs to maintain and equip its forces based on forecasted needs and threats.[44] Our interviewees expressed doubt that there was much input from military units or service arms—for example, the Ground Forces or Navy—about their needs during the SAP's formulation. Rather, these requirements are generally informed by the MoD's 46th Central

---

[39] Janes, 2022b.

[40] Cooper, 2017; Russia subject-matter expert, interview with the authors, November 2022.

[41] Cooper, 2017.

[42] Cooper, 2017.

[43] Cooper, 2017.

[44] V. M. Burenok, ed., *Concept of Justification of Prospective Share of Power Components of the Military Organization of the Russian Federation*, Russian Academy of Missile and Artillery Sciences, 2018.

Research Institute, which is tasked with objectively forecasting requirements. The requirements also reflect input from the VPK, representing Rostec and the defense industry and national security agencies.[45] The MoD then requests a large sum for procurement, with the Ministry of Finance often counterproposing a much more conservative amount, given the constraints of the budget and the macroeconomic forecasts; however, the final word on funding rests with the President.[46]

The most recent SAP (SAP-2027), which was established in 2018 and covers the period from 2018 through 2027, allocates approximately 19 trillion rubles ($280 billion) for modernization and rearmament, and approximately 1 trillion rubles ($15 billion) for storage infrastructure. SAP-2027 was described in our interviews as a shift toward quality over quantity in a move to improve Russia's command, control, communications, and computer platforms and infrastructure for equipment built during the period covered by SAP-2020.[47] SAP-2027 has been paused in light of large Russian equipment losses in 2022 from the war in Ukraine, as discussed later. Although the SAP is classified, press reporting highlights its goals. Priorities of SAP-2027 include the following:

- Ground Forces (Army), 15–25 percent of the allocation
  - tanks: modernization of T-72s, T-80s, and T-90Ms; orders for new weaponry, engines, armor, and a small quantity of T-14s
  - armored fighting vehicles: upgrades to BMP-2s and BMD-2s; procurement of Kurganets-25s, BMP Dragoons, and armored personnel carriers and support vehicles for airborne troops
  - artillery: Uragan-M1 and Tornado-S multiple-launch rocket systems, unmanned aircraft systems for regiments and brigades, precision-guided munitions, mortars, and 2S35 Koalitsiya tracked and wheeled howitzers
- air defense and precision strike, 15–25 percent of the allocation
  - S-300, S-400 long-range surface-to-air missile systems, Iskander-M medium-range ballistic and cruise missile systems, and Pantir-Sm and Buk-M3 short-range systems
- Navy, less than 25 percent of the allocation
  - surface vessels: modernization of smaller Krivak frigates and Karakurt corvettes; procurement of new Gremyashchiy corvettes, Admiral *Grigorovich/Gorshkov*-class frigates; procurement of Kalibr-NK, P-800 Oniks, and Poliment-Redut missiles and K-300P Bastion and BAL coastal defense systems

---

[45] Russia subject-matter expert, interview with the authors, October 2022.

[46] Konstantin Bogdanov, "Signed for 10 Years, Here Is What the New Government Arms Program Is Dedicated to for the Years 2018–2027" ["Подписались на 10 лет Чему посвящена новая госпрограмма вооружений, утвержденная на 2018-2027 годы"], *Izvestiya*, February 28, 2018.

[47] Russia subject-matter expert, interview with the authors, October 2022.

- submarines: modernization of *Antey*-class and *Shchuka-B*-class submarines with Kalibr and P-800 Oniks missiles; procurement of *Yasen-M*-class nuclear attack submarines and *Varshavyanka*-class, *Lada*-class, and *Kalina*-class diesel submarines
- Aerospace Forces (Air Force), 25 percent of the allocation
  - fighters: modernization of Su-30SMs and MiG-31s; procurement of Su-35Ss and MiG-35s
  - bombers: modernization of Su-25s; procurement of Su-34s
  - helicopters: procurement of Mi-28N/NMs, Kamov Ka-52 Katran/Alligators, and Ka-52K Katran naval variants
  - transport: procurement of Ilyushin IL-476s, IL-76MDs, and IL-106 Yermaks
- Strategic Rocket Forces, residual of the allocation[48]
  - missiles: RS-24 Yars and RS-28 Sarmat intercontinental ballistic missiles (ICBMs) to replace silo-based systems
  - Avangard System: 15Yu71 hypersonic glide vehicles to be delivered on the newly deployed RS-28 Sarmat ICBMs.[49]

The SAP is an aspirational document. Although it is framed as a ten-year plan, it is often overwritten with a new SAP within five years of its undertaking. Moreover, many of the contracts that the MoD signs with defense firms are for shorter terms than five to ten years. This practice provides some degree of flexibility for the MoD, but at the expense of defense firms, which have trouble hiring the right personnel and making long-term investment decisions.[50] Regardless, the MoD rarely cancels programs, which is likely because of pressure from higher echelons of the state. Most often, it will postpone such programs for years or even a decade.[51] Rostec, the state-owned defense holding company, appears to have a powerful lobby—perhaps even more powerful than the military—and this may further explain why the MoD prefers to postpone programs rather than cancel them outright.[52]

Postponement Preferred to Canceling Programs

Over the past 30 years Russia has opted to postpone most weapon programs rather than cancel them outright. Many of Russia's more recent systems, such as the Kh-101 air-launched cruise missile and the Kalibr sea-launched cruise missile, were designed in the late 1980s but

---

[48] Funding for the maintenance, modernization, and procurement of nuclear munitions is specified in one of National Defense's subchapters; specifically, Nuclear Weapons Complex (subchapter 206, which is described in the "Budgeting and Execution" section). Missiles, rockets, and hypersonic weapon systems are funded through the SDO and SAP.

[49] Connolly and Boulégue, 2018.

[50] Russia subject-matter expert, interview with the authors, October 2022.

[51] Aleksandr Golts, "Russia's Rubezh Ballistic Missile Disappears off the Radar," *Eurasia Daily Monitor*, Vol. 14, No. 119, September 27, 2017.

[52] Russia subject-matter expert, interview with the authors, October 2022.

then delayed for more than a decade after the Soviet Union's collapse.[53] Occasionally, Russia's leadership will cancel a weapon program or platform, typically to conserve resources for other programs that are deemed more important. Leadership will also do so if there are multiple issues at the prototype stage or if transitioning to the new system would be prohibitively expensive.

The Russian Ground Forces have seen both major delays and major cancellations. For example, the T-14 Armata tank was announced decades ago as a modern replacement for Russia's tank force, which consists of modernized T-72s, T-90s, and legacy T-80s. In 2014, it was announced that 2,300 T-14 Armatas would be delivered by 2020.[54] This delivery never occurred, for several reasons. The Armata, while advanced, had several technical problems, and firms in Russia faced expensive challenges trying to mass-produce it. Russia had also been relying on large numbers of Armata exports to such countries as India, which backed out of the deal for unknown reasons. Although there has been no official cancellation notice, the Armata program is likely slowly ending; Russia's military is not advocating for it, and only 40 tanks will have been delivered by 2023.[55] More than half of Russia's tank force has been destroyed in Ukraine.[56] It is not known what the replacement tank variant will ultimately be—whether Russia opts to mass-produce cheaper T-72 variants with some sort of improved protection measures or to dig deep and find the funds for a more modern tank. The same company, Uralvagonzavod, produces both T-72 and Armata tanks.

The Russian Navy's surface fleet has seen more than its share of financial woes and project cancellations in the past 30 years as Russia has diverted most of the Navy's funds into attack and ballistic missile submarines. This makes it an exception to the identified trend of Russian leaders preferring not to cancel projects outright. Russia has commissioned several new surface ships in the past decade, mostly smaller green water ships that are capable of launching the Kalibr sea-launched cruise missile. Since 2018, Russia has canceled many of its larger blue water surface ships, such as the Project 23560 nuclear-powered cruiser and the Project 22350M frigate. The cancellation of the 22350M made one Russian defense company, the Northern Design Bureau, financially unstable.[57] Russia's government is currently deciding on two competing designs for the next-generation aircraft carrier from the Nevsky Design

---

[53] Center for Strategic and International Studies, "Missiles of Russia," webpage, August 10, 2021.

[54] "20 Trillion Rubles Down the Drain. Largest State Arms Production Program in Russian History Halted Due to Failures in Ukraine" ["20 триллионов на ветер. Крупнейшая в российской истории госпрограмма производства оружия остановлена из-за провалов в Украине"], *Moscow Times*, November 11, 2022.

[55] "20 Trillion Rubles Down the Drain," 2022; Global Defense Corp., "Undignified Death of T-14 Armata Main Battle Tank," February 21, 2020.

[56] Stijn Mitzer and Jakub Janovsky, "Attack on Europe: Documenting Russian Equipment Losses During the 2022 Russian Invasion of Ukraine," Oryx, February 24, 2022.

[57] "Northern Design Bureau Suspended Work on a Prototype Nuclear Destroyer" ["Северное ПКБ приостановило работу над перспективным атомным эсминцем"], Interfax, April 18, 2020.

Bureau and the Krylov State Research Center.[58] In the meantime, Russia's government has authorized another service overhaul for Russia's sole remaining aircraft carrier, the aging and accident-prone *Kuznetsov*, which will have its service life extended beyond 2030.[59] Russia's 2014 invasion of Ukraine led Kyiv to instate an arms embargo to Russia. As a result, Ukrainian defense firms would no longer sell some gas turbine engines that Russia needed for two guided missile frigates (Project 22350 and Project 11356), causing delays until a domestic manufacturer, Saturn, could create a domestic version of the engine.[60]

Russia's aerospace industry has seen its share of changes in the post-Soviet era. In the Russian Air Force, one of Russia's two leading fighter aircraft designers, the Mikoyan and Gurevich (MiG) design bureau (which was founded in 1939), fell on hard times in the early 2000s. MiG had developed its most modern aircraft, the MiG-35 multirole fighter jet, but no orders were ever placed. Other projects were also passed over in favor of MiG's competitor Sukhoi, a company that acquired several billion-dollar contracts for the Su-30, Su-35, Su-35, and Su-57 fighter jets. MiG was thought to be surviving largely on revenues from exports, the repair and maintenance of those exports, and the remaining MiG fighter jets in Russia's inventory.[61] MiG was rumored to be developing a new "sixth-generation" fighter jet, sometimes identified as the MiG-41, but references to the project have mostly disappeared in recent years. This has led some observers to wonder whether the project ended in the research and development phase.[62] As a result of MiG's financial problems, Russia's government ordered it to merge with Sukhoi in 2022 to preserve the capital and intellectual expertise of both companies. Russia-based analysts who study the country's aerospace program did not view this merger as a bad thing. In their view, Russia's defense budget (and need for airframes) was much smaller than in Soviet times, and the defense budget could no longer accommodate both MiG and Sukhoi.[63] Curiously, the CEO of Sukhoi was terminated despite successful programs under his tenure, and the CEO of MiG was brought in to lead the newly merged company. Some in Russia speculated that cronyism, not best business principles, played a part in this decision.[64]

There is no competition among Russia's fleet of strategic bombers, all of which are manufactured by Tupolev. As for transport aircraft, the Antonov joint venture company that had

---

[58] Atle Staalesen, "Putin Takes a Look at New Aircraft Carrier," *Barents Observer*, January 10, 2020.

[59] Mykhailo Samus, "Russia Postpones Future Aircraft Carrier Program," *Eurasia Daily Monitor*, Vol. 15, No. 69, May 7, 2018.

[60] Sam LaGrone, "Russia Navy Faces Surface Modernization Delays Without Ukrainian Engines, Officials Pledge to Sue," USNI News, June 10, 2015.

[61] Matthew Bodner, "Russia's Once-Mighty Fighter Jet Firm MiG Struggling as Rivals Make Gains," *Moscow Times*, July 2, 2015.

[62] Valery Ageev, "MiG-41: Real Breakthrough or Speculation" ["Миг-41: Реальный Прорыв Или Спекуляция"], *Nezavisimoe Voennoe Obozrenie*, September 17, 2020.

[63] Igor Rozin, "Why Has Russia Merged Sukhoi and MiG Corporations into One?" *Russia Beyond*, April 8, 2021.

[64] Bodner, 2015.

made a variety of these systems was broken apart in legal proceedings after the 2014 invasion of Ukraine, a casualty of the severing of ties between the company's Russian and Ukrainian businesses. Many Russian and Ukrainian defense firms had deep ties or were integrated during the Soviet era, and severing these relationships has caused production problems in both countries. Such Russian companies as Ilyushin are trying to fill the gap domestically with the planned PAK VTA heavy transport aircraft, which were designed to replace the An-124.

Although Russia's nuclear forces are the highest priority for protection, even this sector has experienced cancellations and postponements, usually when systems are redundant or when Russia wants to fund a more modern delivery vehicle. By 2016, Russian leaders stopped discussing the RS-26 Rubezh ICBM program despite years of public rollouts, leading observers to conclude that it had been canceled or postponed indefinitely in favor of another ICBM program, the Sarmat heavy ICBM.[65] In 2017, Russian leaders announced the cancellation of the Barguzin rail-mobile ballistic missile system.[66] At the time, there was no explanation for the cancellation, but one year later, President Putin unveiled a suite of new nuclear weapon systems. This move indicates that both the Rubezh and Barguzin programs were canceled because of redundancy and to make room in the budget. In 2018, Russia announced a suite of new nuclear and dual-capable missiles, including the Avanguard hypersonic glide vehicle, the Tsirkon hypersonic antiship cruise missile, the Poseidon nuclear-powered underwater vehicle, the Avangard hypersonic glide vehicle, the Kinzhal air-launched ballistic missile, and the Burevestnik nuclear-powered ground-launched cruise missile.[67]

These postponements and cancellations often disrupt planned SAPs. To account for these disruptions, new SAPs with a new agenda and timeline are created before the planned period of performance of the original SAP ends. There does not appear to be a formal process that reviews where the previous SAP failed and why, although there may be an internal process that is not visible publicly. By announcing a new SAP before the official end of the predecessor SAP, postponements are quietly built into the new program and canceled projects disappear.

Impact of Russia's War on Ukraine

Russia's invasion of Ukraine has shifted Russia's thinking on both military procurement and its short-term needs. In November 2022, the Kremlin paused SAP-2027, committing the annual SDO to meeting the needs of Russia's war in Ukraine, most likely for ground force weapons and equipment.[68] Any future SAP is practically frozen until Russia can deter-

---

[65] Golts, 2017.

[66] Maxim Starchak, "Russia Terminates Development of New Rail-Mobile Ballistic Missile," *Eurasia Daily Monitor*, Vol. 14, No. 162, December 13, 2017.

[67] Edward Geist and Dara Massicot, "Understanding Putin's Nuclear 'Superweapons,'" *SAIS Review of International Affairs*, Vol. 39, No. 2, Summer–Fall 2019.

[68] Aleksei Nikolski, Dmitry Grinkevich, and Irinia Sidorkova, "The Authorities Have Revised the Principles of Procurement for the Needs of the Armed Forces" ["Власти пересмотрели принципы закупок для

mine its acquisition needs on the basis of its experiences in Ukraine.[69] Its losses over the course of the first six months of the conflict, particularly to its armored vehicles, tanks, self-propelled artillery, military trucks, and helicopters, may necessitate an emphasis on *quantity* over quality in preparation for a large-scale *land* war. This would represent a diversion from the original intent of SAP-2027, which had focused on modernizing the forces equally. The Navy, Air Force, and Strategic Rocket Forces have fared better than the Ground Forces in the war, so Russia is likely to prioritize restocking its precision-guided munitions, building or modernizing its tanks and infantry fighting vehicles (but not necessarily constructing newer models, such as the T-90M or Armata), and postponing expensive unmanned aerial systems in favor of cheaper, more disposable versions.[70] Iranian Shahed drones' entrance into the war in Ukraine highlights Russia's shifting emphasis on cheaper, more asymmetrical methods, albeit at the expense of such defense industry players as Rostec, which would prefer that the MoD finance more-expensive projects.[71] Russia is said to be seeking additional artillery munitions from North Korea, and Chinese protective gear has reportedly been provided to some mobilized Russian soldiers.[72]

A year into the war, Russia's defense industrial base was struggling to replenish high expenditures of munitions, including bullets, artillery shells, and missiles, although some factories are working around the clock. Under mobilization laws that took effect in September and October 2022, the Kremlin can exert new authorities to command the industrial base to fulfill domestic contracts more quickly and to pause export contracts, if needed. Russia's Minister of Defense Sergei Shoigu has also announced that the SDO for 2023 will be 50-percent larger, allowing for maximum production of weapon systems to equip and maintain military units at 97-percent operability.[73]

However, more pressure does not guarantee that key factories—configured for peacetime production—can rapidly comply with increased wartime output in the near term. President Putin has put public pressure on his prime minister and defense minister to improve the quality of products delivered to Russian troops in Ukraine. In what could be considered an ad hoc approach to oversight, Russia's former president Dmitry Medvedev traveled to Uralvagonzavod, Russia's main tank factory, to personally convey the urgency of compliance, grimly recounting his message on social media afterward:

нужд вооруженных сил"], *Vedomosti*, November 11, 2022.

[69] Nikolski, Grinkevich, and Sidorkova, 2022.

[70] Russia subject-matter expert, interview with the authors, October 2022.

[71] Russia subject-matter expert, interview with the authors, October 2022.

[72] Karoun Demirjian, Karen DeYoung, and Ellen Nakashima, "North Korea Covertly Supplying Russia with Artillery Rounds, U.S. Says," *Washington Post*, November 2, 2022; Dmitri [@wartranslated], "Continuation of the story with mobilized soldiers from the Moscow region aggressively talking to the officer about their lack of proper equipment and treatment," post on the X platform, November 13, 2022.

[73] Meduza Project, "Russia Will Increase Funding for State Defense Orders by One and a Half Times" ["Россия увеличит финансирование гособоронзаказа в полтора раза"], November 30, 2022c.

The goal has been set for a scrupulous execution of the government's defense contracts in all of its key parameters, [and] prevention of disruptions in the supply of equipment. Attention has been drawn to the fact that all contractors could be held to account, including on criminal charges. . . . Supervision over the execution will continue.[74]

Budgeting and Execution

Russia's Budget Code outlines the budget's chapters. For example, Chapter 1 is Revenues, Chapter 2 is Expenditures, Chapter 2.1 is General Government, Chapter 2.2 is National Defense, and so on. These chapters direct how the appropriated money should be spent. Although the chapters ensure that budget funds serve different purposes with different colors of money, it looks increasingly likely that sequestration of funds across chapters and subchapters is becoming more common in wartime. The following subchapters fall under National Defense:

- 201: Armed Forces of the Russian Federation—This subchapter includes funding for the Armed Forces and the General Staff, specifically for personnel, operation and maintenance, and modernization expenses across all the services. The classified portion of this subchapter is assumed to constitute two-thirds of the SDO for procurement every year.
- 202: Modernization of the Armed Forces—This subchapter was introduced in 2007 but has not been used.
- 203: Mobilization and Pre-Conscription Training—This subchapter includes funding for military recruitment and conscription centers. After the September 2022 announcement of mobilization for the war in Ukraine, social media videos of conscription centers began to show how limited the resources for mobilization had been, perhaps exposing the ineffectiveness of this funding or even underlying corruption and embezzlement.[75]
- 204: Mobilization of the Economy—This subchapter is believed to be an allocation to the VPK to prepare and manage the defense industry for mobilization. This allocation is relatively small, so it may serve as some form of retainer for defense industry firms.[76]
- 205: Participating in Collective Peacekeeping Agreements—This is funding for Russia's peacekeeping missions, such as in Sudan in 2012–2014. It is not funded every year.
- 206: Nuclear Weapons Complex—This is funding for the maintenance, modernization, procurement, research, and development of nuclear munitions by Rosatom. The funding is completely classified, but given the size of the appropriation, we can assume that it is used mainly for munitions and warheads. Delivery systems, such as the Avangard

---

[74] Eric Tegler, "A New Kremlin 'Committee' Won't Accelerate Production of Weapons for Russian Troops in Ukraine," *Forbes*, October 26, 2022.

[75] Russia subject-matter expert, interview with the authors, October 2022.

[76] Russia subject-matter expert, interview with the authors, October 2022.

hypersonic glide vehicle and the Kinzhal air-launched Iskander, are likely procured by the Strategic Rocket Forces and Ground Forces, respectively, through the SDO.[77]

- 207: International Military-Technical Cooperation—This is funding for military-technical cooperation agreements, such as arms transfers to other states.
- 208: Research and Development—This funding is mainly for the SDO. The appropriation accounts for approximately the remaining third of the SDO's budget.
- 209: Other Expenditures—This subchapter generally covers funding for agencies involved in miliary programs, such as the Federal Agency for Special Construction and the Federal Agency for the Delivery of Armaments. For the MoD, this allocation is used for other targeted defense programs.[78] It increased exponentially in the 2023 budget (see Table 3.3); therefore, the amount likely serves some purpose for the war in Ukraine.

TABLE 3.3

Subchapters of National Defense in Russia's 2021 and 2023 Budgets

Title	Chapter Number	2021 Budget (U.S.$ billions)	Percentage Classified	2023 Budget (U.S.$ billions)	Percentage Classified
Armed Forces of the Russian Federation	2.201	30.98	56.9	34.54	55.7
Modernization of the Armed Forces	2.202	—	N/A	—	N/A
Mobilization and Pre-Conscription Training	2.203	0.10	0.0	0.24	0.0
Mobilization of the Economy	2.204	0.04	100	0.04	100
Participation in Collective Peacekeeping Agreements	2.205	—	N/A	—	N/A
Nuclear Weapons Complex	2.206	0.61	100	0.67	100
International Military-Technical Cooperation	2.207	0.20	56.7	0.20	52.9
Research and Development	2.208	5.00	94.7	5.56	94.1
Other Expenditures	2.209	5.41	83.5	26.43	90.8
National Defense chapter total	2.2	42.35	65.3	67.68	72.8

SOURCE: Features data from Russian Treasury, 2012-2021; Dmitriev, 2022.

NOTE: N/A = not applicable because the subchapter has not received budget allocations. The table does not include 2022 budget numbers because the Ministry of Finance and Ministry of Treasury have limited the publication of these data and have discontinued publication of the implementation data for the 2022 budget, an operations security move because of the war in Ukraine. Ruble-to-dollar conversions use the average 2021 exchange rate of 73.6 rubles per U.S. dollar.

---

[77] Russia subject-matter expert, interview with the authors, October 2022.

[78] Julian Cooper, *Russian Military Expenditure: Data, Analysis and Issues*, Swedish Defense Research Agency, September 2013.

Russia's national defense appropriation grew by 1.4 trillion rubles in nominal terms (around $19 billion) from the 2022 budget to the 2023 budget, according to media reporting, while the portion of the National Defense chapter budget that was classified increased from 65 percent to 73 percent, likely as a result of operations security measures because of the war in Ukraine. Subchapter 209 (Other Expenditures) was the main driver of growth; the classified portion of that budget increased nearly sixfold, from 295.7 billion rubles in 2022 to 1.7 trillion rubles in 2023. Finance Minister Anton Siluanov said that support for Russia's annexations in Ukraine was included in the budget but that spending on the war would not be made public.[79] Other areas of the budget (including regional budgets) have also increased and have adopted a similar opacity; in some cases, these appropriations may be used to compensate the families of those killed in action in Ukraine.[80]

The war has triggered force majeure in Russia's budget. Moreover, sequestration of funds seems almost certain across the National Defense subchapters—and across the budget overall—to support the war, and the government has the broad power to do it.[81] For example, in October 2022, the Duma Committee on Budget and Taxes hosted Vladmir Mau, head of the Russian Presidential Academy of National Economy and Public Administration, who recommended a macroeconomic forecast in the budget for "economic mobilization."[82]

Oversight

The MoD produces audit reports on defense spending. These audits are reportedly checked by the Federal Agency for State Property Management, which controls some of the largest defense industrial holdings. The reports are then sent to the Accounts Chamber, the independent government entity responsible for financial control and auditing budget funds. However, the extent to which the Accounts Chamber scrutinizes classified information is unknown.[83] We assume that the Accounts Chamber analyzes the classified portions of the National Defense chapter and that this analysis is seen only by the State Duma Committee on Defense, which is composed of approximately 20 deputies who are assigned to review defense

[79] Dmitriev, 2022.

[80] Antonina Asanova, "Pay for My Iskanders: How Russia Spends the Profits Received from the Oil and Gas Trade on the War: A Study by *Novaya Gazeta Europe*" ["Оплатите мои «Искандеры» Как Россия тратит на войну сверхдоходы, полученные от торговли нефтью и газом: исследование «Новой газеты. Европа"], *Novaya Gazeta Europe*, July 11, 2022.

[81] Russia subject-matter expert, interview with the authors, October 2022; Nikolski, Grinkevich, and Sidorkova, 2022.

[82] Meduza Project, "Russian Officials Are Constantly Talking About the Transition to a 'Mobilization Economy'—as in the Years of the Great Patriotic War. Is That Really Happening?" ["Российские чиновники постоянно говорят о переходе к «мобилизационной экономике»—как в годы Великой Отечественной войны. Это правда происходит?"], November 21, 2022a.

[83] Transparency International Defense and Security, 2019–2020, comprehensiveness indicator (28a).

and security spending. However, it is unclear whether this committee receives the full MoD audit reports from prior years for comparison.[84]

Not all deputies in the Duma have access to classified information. In the past, opposition parties had few or no deputies with access, which might explain some of the larger oversight issues at play.[85] This trend is likely stronger now, with even fewer members of the opposition in the Duma. The Duma Committee on Budget and Taxes does invite economic experts from research institutions and universities to assess the unclassified portions of the budget.[86]

Access to classified information as an employee of the Russian state comes with increased wages and/or other benefits. Therefore, there is an incentive both to have access to classified information and to classify more information, which further limits transparency.[87] Furthermore, the MoD is allocated resources each year for personnel and operations based on enlistment statistics, which incentivizes the ministry to exaggerate the number of active and reserve personnel in its units. Because the government recently classified all manner of information about the Armed Forces' structure as state secrets, uncleared personnel in the government will have no ability to audit the military's personnel billets and confirm these staffing claims. The former head of the Accounts Chamber, Alexei Kudrin, has complained repeatedly that his agency has not been able to examine defense spending to the extent that he would like and that the MoD has always leaned on national security as an excuse for this lack of transparency.[88]

In general, however, all recipients of budget funds are required to prepare monthly, quarterly, and annual reports on the implementation of funds, balances, cash flows, and other relevant information for their respective budget administrators (e.g., the Deputy Minister for Financial and Economic Matters in the MoD). The administrators submit the consolidated reports to the Treasury and a prior-year report on the use of funds to the Accounts Chamber no later than April 1. The Treasury submits the consolidated reports to the Ministry of Finance, which prepares an annual report on the implementation of the budget. The ministry submits its annual report to the Duma no later than the draft budget submission; that report represents the *reporting* phase of the budget process. The Accounts Chamber submits its conclusions and queries from its audit to the budget administrators no later than June 1 and then to the Duma no later than September 1; this audit constitutes the *audit* phase of the budget process. (See Figure 3.1, earlier in this chapter, for a visualization of the process.)[89]

---

[84] Cooper, 2017; Transparency International Defense and Security, 2019–2020, parliamentary scrutiny indicator (28b).

[85] Cooper, 2017.

[86] Cooper, 2017.

[87] Cooper, 2017.

[88] Russia subject-matter expert, interview with the authors, October 2021.

[89] Budget.gov.ru, "The Procedure and Terms for Compiling, Submitting, External Verification, Review and Approval of Budget Reporting, Unified Portal of the Budget System of the Russian Federation" ["Порядок

Analysis of Russia's Defense Budgeting Process

Strengths

Planning and budgeting appear to be the stronger aspects of Russia's PPBE-like process. Up until the war in Ukraine, resources were budgeted in a fiscally responsible way within the Ministry of Finance and the Ministry of Economic Development's macroeconomic framework. Additionally, the use of fiscal rules to divert oil and natural gas revenues to pay down deficits and build up a national wealth fund has proven to be pragmatic not only in preparing Russia for fiscal hardship but also in limiting the exposure of its sovereign debt to foreign sanctions. This fiscally sound budgeting practice has somewhat softened the impact of the 2022 sanctions packages against Russia.

Planning and budgeting for defense are closely linked by the SAP and the SDO, respectively, but there is room for long-term adjustments. In theory, the SAP is a ten-year military procurement plan, and the SDO is the annual allocation needed to pay for procurement over the course of those ten years. In practice, however, the SAP is revised every five years or so, which means that contracts between the MoD and the defense industrial base tend to be shorter than ten years. Limiting the time frame for these contracts can give the MoD some flexibility, but to the detriment of defense industrial firms' long-term planning. That said, outright cancellations of MoD military acquisition programs are rare. Because much of its budget is classified, there is some debate about how well developed the SAP really is, and the major stakeholders—the president and his Security Council—seem to play outsized roles in defining defense spending throughout the process.

Russia's invasion of Ukraine has shown that Russia can rapidly pivot to fulfill different military procurement needs, albeit under extreme pressure. In November 2022, Russia suspended SAP-2027 and announced that it would commit a significantly larger SDO to the war. Several reports suggested some forms of mobilization of the defense industrial base in fall 2022 as Russia created a "government coordination council" to expedite the resupply of Russia's military.[90] Uralvagonzavod, the major producer of tanks and armored fighting vehicles, instituted overtime shifts, weekend work, increased pay, and even hired prisoners to serve their sentences by working at the plant.[91] Having to rely on prisoners instead of being able to incentivize the local population may be a troubling indicator for the long-term health of Russia's defense industrial labor pool. Another example of mobilizing the defense industrial base

---

и сроки составления, представления, внешней проверки, рассмотрения и утверждениябюджетной отчетности, Единый портал бюджетной системы российской федерации"], webpage, undated-c.

[90] Pavel Luzin, "The Kremlin's Economic Mobilization," *Eurasia Daily Monitor*, Vol. 19, No. 161, October 31, 2022; Maxim Starchak, "Missed Targets: The Struggles of Russia's Missile Industry," Center for European Policy Analysis, June 27, 2022.

[91] "Employees of Uralvagonzavod Will Be Transferred to Overtime Work Due to the State Defense Order" ["Сотрудников Уралвагонзавода переведут на сверхурочную работу из-за гособоронзаказа"], *Kommersant*, August 31, 2022; Meduza Project, "250 Convicts Will Serve Forced-Labor Sentences at Nizhny Tagil Tank and Armored-Vehicle Construction Plant," November 29, 2022b.

is the Kalashnikov Concern, which was appointed by the Ministry of Industry and Trade to be the main coordinator for the delivery of body armor, helmets, and small arms to the MoD to help remedy the deficit of equipment and poor conditions that Russian troops shared on social media.[92]

Challenges

Russia's war in Ukraine has exposed serious challenges in its PPBE-like process. As we noted earlier, there is a major disconnect among the planning and budgeting of funds, programming, and, ultimately, execution. Failures of oversight and quality control appear at every level among equipment and personnel in Ukraine, from deficient federal auditing to equipment leaving factories in an unacceptable condition for operational use. In peacetime, these oversight and quality-control failures are often hidden from Russia's lawmakers and the public; but during the war, they are evidenced by poor delivery performance and quality of equipment. At the most basic level, uniforms go missing or are never delivered, while troops receive expired rations and faulty equipment.[93] The anecdotal nature of these accounts precludes an assessment of how widespread the phenomenon is.

The fall 2022 mobilization is another example of failed oversight and application of a PPBE process. Russia's military was unprepared for this event after largely neglecting the mobilization system for a decade, including hidden graft. Images and videos of dire conditions at military recruitment commissariats and among the mobilized in occupied Ukraine lay bare the disconnect between the planning and budgeting of defense funds on one hand—in this case, for mobilization—and the programming and actual execution of those funds on the other hand, especially for mobilization.[94] In the early months of mobilization, soldiers lacked proper uniforms and shoes, and local governors and mayors were made responsible for outfitting units from their regions, with highly variable results. The mobilized were given old, faulty rifles instead of properly-cared-for equipment. Such a disconnect has led to dire consequences: The announced mobilization of 300,000 men triggered the emigration of an estimated 260,000 men from Russia to neighboring countries; combined, the mobilization

---

[92] "'Kalashnikov' Was Appointed to Lead the Supply of Equipment, the Source Said," RIA Novosti, November 13, 2022.

[93] According to a politician from central Russia, 1.5 million uniforms had gone missing once Russia declared mobilization in fall 2022 ("'Where Did They Disappear To?' Russian MP Says 1.5 Million Military Uniforms Are Missing," *Novaya Gazeta Europe*, October 2, 2022). A photo circulated on social media in July 2022 allegedly showed a captured BMP barrel manufactured incorrectly, with a barrel wall thickness of 8 mm on one side and 11 mm on the other (General M [@GenerMo], "@PhillipsPOBrien @JominiW @noclador @GlasnostGone @DefMon3 perhaps you will be interested, this barrel from the Russian BMP was filmed by Ukrainians," post on the X platform, July 24, 2022). This suggests multiple levels of quality-control problems during production (Cranny-Evans and Ivshina, 2022).

[94] "Russia Sends Mobilized Men to Ukraine Front After Days of Training—Activists," *Moscow Times*, September 27, 2022.

and emigration could have reduced the male labor pool by approximately 2 percent.[95] The Gaidar Institute in Moscow predicts that potential labor shortages affect one-third of industry in Russia.[96] Casualty rates among the mobilized during Russia's winter 2023 offensive are estimated to be in the hundreds per day.[97]

Although Russia's procurement process has been designed to minimize waste and conserve resources, corruption is still rampant. Transparency International rates Russia's defense sector as having a high risk for corruption. Among the reasons listed in the weighted ranking, those closely related to the PPBE process are

1. a lack of independent legislative scrutiny of defense policy
2. a high percentage of defense and national security expenditures cloaked in secrecy
3. a lack of comprehensive data and publicly available audits on defense spending during the budget year
4. a severe lack (or absence) of training on anticorruption measures for military leaders at all levels and an absence of trained professionals deployed to monitor corruption risks in the field
5. little public disclosure of the defense procurement life cycle, from bidding to acquisition decommissioning.[98]

Although many aspects of budgeting and planning have been codified into Russian law on a sound basis, programming, execution, and the institutions responsible for them have been weakened by more than 20 years of state power that has become increasingly concentrated at the executive level. Excessive classification of military details has limited transparency and oversight even within Russia's government. The allocation of budget resources to defense and national security is closely controlled by the president, his Security Council, the MoD, and the defense industrial base; there is ineffectual debate by the legislature and hampered oversight in the Accounts Chamber, let alone in the public and civil society. The list of classified state secrets grew exponentially in 2022, exacerbating the problem, and the prohibition of private citizens from discussing such details as military force structure, ongoing operations, or the defense sector (according to a law that went into effect in December 2022),[99] has made the process even more opaque. Execution of defense spending is then subject to corruption

---

[95] "Factbox: Where Have Russians Been Fleeing to Since Mobilisation Began?" Reuters, October 6, 2022; "Russia's Labor-Starved Economy Pays Price of Putin's Call-Up," Bloomberg News, December 1, 2022.

[96] Gaidar Institute for Economic Policy, "Sergei Tsukhlo Assesses the Labor Deficit in Industry" ["Сергей Цухло Оценил Дефицит Кадров в Промышленности"], November 11, 2022.

[97] Helene Cooper, Eric Schmitt, and Thomas Gibbons-Neff, "Soaring Death Toll Gives Grim Insight into Russian Tactics," *New York Times*, February 2, 2023.

[98] Transparency International Defence and Security, 2019–2020.

[99] "Russia Bans Public Discussion of Army Strategy, Troop Morale, and Mobilization," *Moscow Times*, December 1, 2022.

within the MoD, cronyism throughout the defense industrial base, and a general lack of serious anticorruption measures because senior members of the government benefit financially from much of this malfeasance.[100]

Applicability

Many European countries have some form of medium-term budgetary framework in place with cycles of three years or more, and these practices have influenced Russia's budgeting and planning process. Differences emerge in how a country sets its expenditure ceiling(s), with the understanding that governments have more control over the expenditure side of their budgets than the revenue side (which depends more on the economy). In some countries, there is more detail and control over the expenditure ceiling than in others. For example, Sweden and Finland set central government expenditure ceilings that are not expected to be changed. The Netherlands sets three separate expenditure ceilings: one for the central government, one for pensions, and one for health care. France and the United Kingdom set ministry-level expenditure ceilings that can be changed at the discretion of the government as long as those changes are justified and explained in the budget.[101]

Russia is unique in that it has (on paper) a ten-year SAP supported by a three-year budget—a combination that, in theory, provides a mix of stability and flexibility to the MoD and the defense industry. But, in reality, the SAP is aspirational: Its contracts often fall short, and, in the face of war, it is dispensable. Sometimes, contract failures are the fault of the defense industry, which underperforms in terms of delivery and quality. Sometimes, such failures are the fault of the government, which fails to provide meaningful contracts that would encourage the defense industry to invest more in personnel and technology over a period greater than three years. The result is a system that our interviewees described as "hand-to-mouth" or short-term survival in the defense industrial base.[102]

Lessons from Russia's Defense Budgeting Process

See Table 3.4 for an overview of the lessons learned from our review of Russia's defense budgeting process.

---

[100] Alison Quinn, "Russia's Defence Minister 'Secretly Builds £12 Million Palace,' Say Campaigners," *The Telegraph*, October 29, 2015.

[101] Monika Sherwood, *Medium-Term Budgetary Frameworks in the EU Member States*, European Commission, European Economy Discussion Paper 021, December 2015.

[102] Russia subject-matter experts, interviews with the authors, October 2022; Sherwood, 2015.

Lesson 1: Russia's Institutions Have Been Weakened by an Increasingly Powerful Executive Authority and a Preference for "Power Agencies," Diminishing Key Roles in the PPBE Process

The MoD, VPK, Rostec, the president, and the Security Council all work within the macroeconomic framework of the budget set by the Ministry of Economic Development and Ministry of Finance. At least in peacetime, there is less evidence that the Duma incorporates MoD audit reports into its debates or that it can affect defense spending while passing the budget.[103] Moreover, there is evidence of cronyism between the executive branch and the defense industry, which is made clear by personal relations between President Putin, the Minister of Defense, and the head of Rostec, as well as by large defense industry holdings under the Federal Agency for State Property Management. Fewer legislators than before have access to secret information on defense spending, and fewer—if any—opposition politicians remain in either house of the legislature. Oversight and quality control suffer when relevant bodies cannot gain access to materials and when jobs are at risk when stakeholders voice dissent.

Lesson 2: With Respect to Planning and Programming, the SAP Is an Aspirational, Nonbinding Document That Is Rarely Fulfilled

Russia's SAP documents, though often tied closely to strategy and the threats that Russia faces, remain aspirational and fall short for a variety of reasons. Prior to the war in Ukraine, the SAP was rarely fulfilled because of economic conditions, technical limitations, or competing priorities between the MoD and the defense industry. To date, the most successful SAP was adopted in 2011 and covered the period through 2020; it resulted in significant modernization of the Russian Armed Forces. However, it does not appear that SAP-2020 and SAP-2027 (the current SAP) were geared to the type of war that Russia is fighting in Ukraine, which emphasizes traditional ground forces, precision-guided munitions, and unmanned aerial systems. These faults, again, probably lie in (1) the disconnect between the president and his Security Council and the rest of the government and (2) the lack of preparations needed for a war of this size and its accompanying excessive operational security. This war is not the war that Russia was necessarily planning to fight. As a result, SAP-2027 has been paused, and the SDO is committed to the war that Russia is fighting. This outcome shows that Russia's system can be flexible and change as needed without facing political or legal ramifications. Essentially, Russia's process is planned and stable until it needs to be jettisoned in favor of a "what works now" strategy. However, these rapid shifts will not be easy for the defense base to comply with and will likely harm its long-term health and ability to innovate as funding streams are disrupted and diverted for near-term emergency wartime production.

---

[103] Transparency International Defence and Security, 2019–2020, parliamentary scrutiny indicator (28b).

Lesson 3: Russia's Budget Process Has Been Developed with Best Practices in Mind, but the Execution Invites Corruption

Russia's budgeting process seems logical when considering other countries' best practices. Russia's budget has been based on best practices and recommendations from the IMF and OECD, such as the use of a three-year or medium-term expenditure framework. Moreover, the Ministry of Economic Development and Ministry of Finance produce macroeconomic and socioeconomic forecasts, respectively, and allocate funding annually within reasonable constraints. The Russian government's spending practices are fiscally conservative in that it does not engage in excessive debt spending or foreign borrowing, and it maintains a sovereign wealth fund to manage shocks or unforeseen events. However, execution is a weak point in Russia's system. The system allows for excessive graft and corruption and the delivery of substandard products to the military. Once the MoD receives procurement funding, its execution becomes opaque to multiple parties within Russia and to outside observers. As Transparency International pointed out, there is little training or field oversight of anticorruption practices among military leadership; furthermore, tenders are not open to competition, contracts with defense industry firms are not fully available to the public, and the procurement life cycle of military equipment—from bidding and acquisition to decommissioning—is only partially visible.[104]

Lesson 4: Defense Spending Is Exceedingly Classified, Which Prohibits Necessary and Effective Audits

In 2022, approximately 15 percent of the defense budget was classified; that percentage has risen to nearly 23 percent in the 2023 budget. The National Defense budget chapter alone has gone from 65-percent to 73-percent classified. The war in Ukraine—and government efforts to hide its actions, its missteps, and the casualties of that war—is likely the reason for this increase in classification. The MoD's financial and audit departments do not release public reports on spending. The Accounts Chamber publishes an annual report on the implementation of the budget, which specifies only total defense spending and disaggregated unclassified defense spending. The Accounts Chamber may be the only independent entity with oversight of defense and national security spending, yet its access to classified information is questionable. Alexei Kudrin, the former head of the Accounts Chamber, has complained about a lack of access to classified defense spending. In addition, new laws that classify information on many military topics, including procurement, force structure, and even strategy—compounded by the closure or departure of most independent Russian media outlets—prevent open discussions of these issues in Russia's society and further contribute to a lack of oversight and accountability.

---

[104] Transparency International Defence and Security, 2019–2020, operational and procurement indicators.

TABLE 3.4

Lessons from Russia's Defense Budgeting Process

Theme	Lesson Learned	Description
Decisionmakers and stakeholders	Lesson 1: Russia's institutions have been weakened by an increasingly powerful executive authority and a preference for "power agencies," diminishing key roles in the PPBE process.	Institutions have been weakened by a powerful president and defense industry. The Duma may not fully see or use audited MoD spending reports in debates and has exhibited little influence over final defense spending. The final word on defense spending rests with the president.
Planning and programming	Lesson 2: With respect to planning and programming, the SAP is an aspirational, nonbinding document that is rarely fulfilled.	The SAP is only a plan and can be rapidly jettisoned without political or legal blowback, leaving companies in a vulnerable position over the long term. The SAP has now been paused, and the SDO is being committed to the needs of the war in Ukraine.
Budgeting and execution	Lesson 3: Russia's budget process has been developed with best practices in mind, but the execution invites corruption.	Russia's budget is logically planned and fiscally conservative, but its execution is opaque, disconnected, and prone to corruption. The execution is done with few safeguards, little oversight, and meager quality control.
Oversight	Lesson 4: Defense spending is exceedingly classified, which prohibits necessary and effective audits.	Defense spending is increasingly classified, making oversight elusive. The Accounts Chamber might provide the only independent oversight of MoD spending but might not have the necessary access to classified information. Russian media and society are now legally prohibited from discussing many military topics, exacerbating the situation.

CHAPTER 4

Key Insights from China and Russia Case Studies

The two near-peer case studies presented in this report are integral inputs for the Commission on PPBE Reform to use to respond to questions from Congress about the competitiveness implications of the defense resource planning approaches of strategic competitors. In Chapters 2 and 3, we discussed how China and Russia, respectively, conduct defense resource planning, programming, budgeting, execution, and oversight—and the strengths and challenges of their approaches, albeit with imperfect information.

This final chapter focuses on summary takeaways. As part of this analysis, we used an initial set of standard questions from the commission, focusing on core areas related to resource planning, as a means of ensuring that there would be some ability to compare across cases. The material presented in this chapter, as distilled from Chapters 2 and 3, outlines important themes for the commission to understand when trying to compare the U.S. defense resource planning process with the processes of near-peer competitors. Despite a long list of differences in the features of China's, Russia's, and U.S. defense resource planning processes, these near-peer case studies suggest several insights that are germane for the United States, as presented below.

The following section on key insights consolidates the strengths, challenges, and lessons outlined in the case studies in this volume. The concluding section on applicability speaks directly to the commission's mandate—and to the potential utility of these insights for DoD's PPBE processes.

Key Insights

China and Russia Make Top-Down Decisions About Priorities and Risks but Face Limitations in Implementation

Senior leaders in these countries have the authority to make top-down decisions, but realizing returns on those decisions is contingent on key social, economic, and other factors. In China, modernization in such areas as jet engines, semiconductors, and hypersonics has not yielded consistent outcomes; other determinative factors are long-term investment stability, innovation enablers, and a workforce with relevant expertise.

Russia's invasion of Ukraine has shown that Russia can rapidly pivot to fulfill different military procurement needs, albeit under extreme pressure. In November 2022, Russia suspended SAP-2027 and announced that it would commit a significantly larger SDO to the war. However, Russia's new mobilization laws, which were meant to respond to wartime needs more rapidly, confronted limitations in industrial capacity, supply chain reliability, and the ability to call up required manpower even through conscription.

China and Russia Make Long-Term Plans but Have Mechanisms for Changing Course in Accordance with Changing Priorities

In China and Russia, centralized decisionmaking can reduce the friction associated with course corrections, although the need to make hard choices is likely lower in China than in Russia because of China's economic growth over recent decades.

Especially in China, Political Leaders Provide Stable and Sustained Long-Term Support for Military Modernization Priorities

The lack of political opposition, the high degree of alignment between CMC and senior CCP leaders, and the sheer scale of military investment over decades have facilitated the stable planning and long-term investments that are essential for making progress toward complex modernization priorities. The synchronization of defense plans with budgets has offered long-term benefits to China's military modernization. In contrast, Russia has a ten-year SAP supported by a three-year budget—a combination that, in theory, balances stability with flexibility for the MoD and the defense industry. But in reality, the SAP is aspirational and has been rapidly jettisoned without political or legal blowback, leaving companies in a vulnerable position over the long term.

China and Russia Have Weak Mechanisms for Avoiding Graft or Ensuring Transparency, Efficiency, Effectiveness, and Quality Control in PPBE-Like Processes

The power dynamics and the structures of decisionmaking in these countries provide limited guardrails for ensuring efficiency, effectiveness, or oversight of investments. Oversight is essential to control corruption and ensure proper budget execution. However, in China, there is weak oversight and the potential for corruption, misuse of funds, and waste. China's budgeting processes are hampered by clientelism (bribery), patronage (favoritism), and other forms of corruption that pervade the defense industries. Powerful SOEs continue to operate in a highly inefficient and wasteful manner, partly because of the political power they exert. Similarly, in Russia, execution of defense spending is subject to corruption within the MoD, cronyism throughout the defense industrial base, and a general lack of serious anticorruption measures.

Reforms in China and Russia Have Been Designed to Increase Oversight of Resource Allocation Processes

In recent years, both countries have recognized the inefficiencies and the limited avenues for competing voices in their top-down budget processes. Both countries have looked to other international models, including that of the United States, for lessons on the development and implementation of budget reforms.

Chinese officials have sought to imitate some practices that are commonly used in Western countries to improve their government's ability to execute budgets. In accordance with centrally directed reforms to all branches of the government, the PLA has carried out multiple rounds of reforms in its budgeting and financial system. Moreover, Chinese leaders have long recognized that the military's budget system, like that of the government overall, suffers from severe problems related to corruption and weak accountability, owing in part to the country's adherence to outdated centralized budgetary practices in which most economic decisions are made by high-level government authorities instead of market participants.

Russia's budget has been based on best practices and recommendations from the IMF and OECD, such as the use of a three-year or medium-term expenditure framework. In addition, the Ministry of Economic Development and the Ministry of Finance produce macroeconomic and socioeconomic forecasts, respectively, and allocate funding annually within reasonable constraints. The Russian government's spending practices are fiscally conservative in that it does not engage in excessive debt spending or foreign borrowing, and it maintains a sovereign wealth fund to manage shocks or unforeseen events. Although Russia's budget process has been developed with best practices in mind, budget execution is done with few safeguards, little oversight, and meager quality control.

Applicability of These Insights to DoD's PPBE System

Although the 2022 NDS calls out China and Russia as posing particular challenges to the United States and the international order, the nature of the challenges posed are distinct and situationally dependent. China and Russia have unique histories, economic conditions, industrial capacities, and military capabilities; thus, they pose unique challenges to the United States. Societal fundamentals for building military capability are critical factors in determining the success of military modernization; therefore, it is unclear how much success can be meaningfully attributed to resource planning processes. Additional critical inputs to success include the following:

- workforce capacity, capabilities, and productivity
- scale and focus of defense investment over time
- industrial capacity and capability
- industrial policy
- innovation policy.

China and Russia are also both extraordinarily different from the United States in political culture, governance structure, values, and strategic orientation. China and Russia have demonstrated that strong central authority (without opposition) can provide long-term planning that aligns resources to priorities and redirects resources to meet changing needs, but there are constraints and trade-offs that come with a top-down approach. A top-down approach can hamper innovation and yield weak mechanisms for oversight and quality control of budget execution.

Given this context, the lessons for U.S. PPBE reform efforts cannot be directly applicable. In addition, there is immense information asymmetry regarding what little we understand and know from open-source reporting on China's and Russia's budgetary processes versus the abundance of critiques in open-source reporting on the U.S. PPBE process. The risk is that China's and Russia's processes may sound more ideal because of a lack of publicly available information about execution. Despite these differences, the case studies suggest several considerations that are relevant for the United States.

The applicability of lessons, mostly from China, will invariably be constrained by the differences between the political systems of the United States and China. DoD will not likely find any simple way of replicating China's advantages by imitation, given the stark differences between the governmental systems of the United States and China. However, finding analogous measures to achieve similar effects could be worthwhile. In particular, two types of measures could have beneficial effects on DoD budgeting practices: (1) finding ways to ensure sustained, consistent funding for priority projects over many years and (2) delegating more authority and granting greater flexibility to project and program managers—without compromising accountability—so that they can make changes to stay in alignment with guidance as technologies and programs advance.

Russia can be fiscally conservative at the federal level, avoiding deficits and engaging in little foreign borrowing, and its defense acquisition plans are often closely tied to military strategy and defense needs. However, opacity in multiple parts of Russia's PPBE-like process—compounded by insufficient oversight—often perpetuates corruption and generates outputs of varying quality from the defense industry. Although there have been attempts to reduce systemic graft and corruption in the past decade, the war in Ukraine has revealed these efforts to be insufficient. Furthermore, the desire for a well-oiled defense industrial base often collides with the excessive concentration of power in Russia's executive branch and the informal practices that make business possible in modern Russia. Russia's PPBE-like process does not allow sufficient oversight to ensure that it works effectively or produces uniformly high-quality products.

Despite the frequent public discussion in the United States that oversight adds time to DoD's PPBE process, it is clear from the experiences of China and Russia that oversight is a critical element that ultimately helps lead to successful capabilities for use during operations and, therefore, should not be haphazardly traded away for speed during resource allocation.

Summary of the Governance and Budgetary Systems of Near-Peer Competitor Case Studies

Finally, we provide a summary of the governance and budgetary systems of the near-peer competitor case studies with the United States for comparison in Tables 4.1 through 4.10.[1] Tables 4.1 and 4.2 show comparisons of the governance structures of the United States, China, and Russia. Tables 4.3 through 4.10 compare the planning, programming, budgeting, and execution processes of the United States, China, and Russia.

TABLE 4.1

Governance: U.S. and Comparative Nation Government Structures and Key Participants

Country	Structure of Government or Political System	Key Governing Bodies and Participants
United States	Federal presidential constitutional republic	• President of the United States • Office of Management and Budget (OMB) • Congress (House of Representatives and Senate) • U.S. Department of Defense (DoD) • Secretary of Defense and senior DoD leadership • Joint Chiefs of Staff
China	Unitary one-party socialist republic	• Politburo Standing Committee • National People's Congress (NPC) • Central Military Commission (CMC)
Russia	Federal semi-presidential republic	• President of Russia • Federal Assembly (State Duma and the Federation Council) • President's Security Council • Ministry of Defense (MoD) • Military-Industrial Commission (VPK) • Rostec (Russian state-owned defense conglomerate headquartered in Moscow)

---

[1] Information presented in these tables is derived from multiple sources and materials reviewed by the authors and cited elsewhere in this report. See the references list for full bibliographic details.

TABLE 4.2

Governance: U.S. and Comparative Nation Spending Controls and Decision Supports

Country	Control of Government Spending	Decision Support Systems
United States	Legislative review and approval of executive budget proposal	• Planning, Programming, Budgeting, and Execution (PPBE) System • Joint Capabilities Integration and Development System (JCIDS) • Defense Acquisition System (DAS)
China	Executive with nominal legislative review and approval	• 2019 Defense White Paper indicated adoption of "demand-oriented planning" and "planning-led" resource allocation
Russia	Executive with assessed nominal legislative review and approval	• Unclear

TABLE 4.3

Planning: U.S. and Comparative Nation Inputs and Outputs

Country	Key Planning Inputs	Selected Planning Outputs
United States	• National Security Strategy • National Defense Strategy • National Military Strategy	• Chairman's Program Recommendations • Defense Planning Guidance • Fiscal Guidance
China	• Five-Year Programs • Military Strategic Guidelines • Other multiyear plans (People's Liberation Army [PLA] five-year professional development plans, etc.) • Annual PLA budget requirements	• Outline of the Five-Year Program for Military Development • Military components of other multiyear plans • Annual PLA budgets
Russia	• State Armaments Program (SAP) procurement plan	• State Defense Order (SDO)

TABLE 4.4

Planning: U.S. and Comparative Nation Strategic Emphasis and Stakeholders

Country	Strategic Planning Emphasis	Planning Stakeholders
United States	2022 National Defense Strategy highlights four priorities: (1) defending the United States, "paced to the growing multi-domain threat posed by the [People's Republic of China (PRC)]"; (2) deterring "strategic attacks against the United States, Allies, and partners"; (3) deterring aggression and being prepared to "prevail in conflict when necessary," with priority placed first on the PRC "challenge in the Indo-Pacific region" and then "the Russia challenge in Europe"; and (4) "building a resilient Joint Force and defense ecosystem."	• Under Secretary of Defense for Policy (lead actor, produces Defense Planning Guidance) • President (National Security Strategy, Fiscal Guidance) • Secretary of Defense (National Defense Strategy, Fiscal Guidance at DoD level) • Chairman of the Joint Chiefs of Staff (CJCS) (National Military Strategy, Chairman's Program Recommendations)
China	Focused, long-term investment for priority projects of high strategic value	• Central Chinese Communist Party leadership • NPC • State Council • Defense-related state-owned enterprises • CMC, senior military leadership
Russia	Closely linked to strategy and national security threats with a recent emphasis on modernization; assessed to be, in part, aspirational	• MoD • Central Research Institute • VPK, representing Rostec, defense industry, and national security agencies

TABLE 4.5

Programming: U.S. and Comparative Nation Resource Allocations and Time Frames

Country	Resource Allocation Decisions	Programming Time Frames
United States	Documented in program objective memorandum (POM) developed by DoD components, reflecting a "systematic analysis of missions and objectives to be achieved, alternative methods of accomplishing them, and the effective allocation of the resources," and reviewed by the Director of Cost Assessment and Program Evaluation (CAPE)	• 5 years
China	Top-down planning from CMC services and commands supplemented by bottom-up requirements submitted by military unit financial departments	• 5 years, sometimes longer
Russia	Top-down planning from Ministry of Defense for the SDO, the annual appropriation for military procurement to meet the requirements of the SAP	• 3 years; nominal 10-year SAP, revised within 5 years in practice

TABLE 4.6

Programming: U.S. and Comparative Nation Stakeholders

Country	Programming Stakeholders
United States	• Director, CAPE (lead actor, provides analytic baseline to analyze POM produced by DoD components, leads program reviews, forecasts resource requirements, and updates the Future Years Defense Program [FYDP]) • DoD components (produce POM, document proposed resource requirements for programs over 5-year time span, which comprises the FYDP) • CJCS (assesses component POMs, provides chairman's program assessment reflecting the extent to which the military departments [MILDEPs] have satisfied combatant command [COCOM] requirements) • Deputy Secretary of Defense (adjudicates disputes through the Deputy's Management Action Groups) • Secretary of Defense (as needed, directs DoD components to execute Resource Management Decision memoranda to reflect decisionmaking during the programming and budget phases)
China	• Ministry of Finance National Defense Department • CMC Logistics Support Department • CMC Strategic Planning Office
Russia	• Ministry of Finance • Ministry of Economic Development • MoD • President's Security Council • VPK

TABLE 4.7

Budgeting: U.S. and Comparative Nation Time Frames and Major Categories

Country	Budget Approval Time Frames	Major Budget Categories
United States	• Annual	• 5 categories: Military Personnel (MILPERS); Operation and Maintenance (O&M); Procurement; Research, Development, Test, and Evaluation (RDT&E); and Military Construction (MILCON)
China	• Annual	• 3 reported categories in defense white papers: personnel, armaments, maintenance and operations
Russia	• Annual	• 9 categories: Armed Forces of the Russian Federation, Modernization of the Armed Forces, Mobilization and Pre-Conscription Training, Mobilization of the Economy, Participation in Collective Peacekeeping Agreements, Nuclear Weapons Complex, International Military-Technical Cooperation, Research and Development, and a category designated for Other Expenditures

TABLE 4.8

Budgeting: Selected U.S. and Comparative Nation Stakeholders

Country	Selected Budgeting Stakeholders
United States	DoD • Under Secretary of Defense (Comptroller) • DoD components and COCOMs Executive Branch • OMB Congress • House Budget Committee • Senate Budget Committee • House Appropriations Committee (Defense Subcommittee) • Senate Appropriations Committee (Defense Subcommittee) • House Armed Services Committee • Senate Armed Services Committee
China	• State Council • NPC • NPC Standing Committee • NPC Finance and Economic Committee
Russia	• Ministry of Finance • Ministry of Economic Development • MoD • President • Federal Assembly (State Duma and the Federation Council) • Accounts Chamber

TABLE 4.9

Execution: U.S. and Comparative Nation Budgetary Flexibilities and Reprogramming

Country	Budgetary Flexibilities and Reprogramming
United States	• Funding availability varies by account type; multiyear or no-year appropriations for limited programs as authorized by Congress • Limited carryover authority in accordance with OMB Circular A-11 • Reprogramming as authorized; four defined categories of reprogramming actions, including prior-approval reprogramming actions—increasing procurement quantity of a major end item, establishing a new program, etc.—which require approval from congressional defense committees • Transfers as authorized through general and special transfer authorities, typically provided in defense authorization and appropriations acts
China	• Some flexibility extended to lower-level decisionmakers to adjust spending and acquisitions; further specifics unclear
Russia	• Signed contract timelines shorter than SAP timelines; provides some degree of flexibility to MoD to realign procurements with changing strategic goals; further specifics unclear

TABLE 4.10

Execution: U.S. and Comparative Nation Assessment

Country	Key Stakeholders in Execution Assessment
United States	• Under Secretary of Defense (Comptroller) • DoD component comptrollers and financial managers • Department of the Treasury • Government Accountability Office • OMB • Defense Finance and Accounting Service
China	• Military Expenditure Performance Management system; guideline-driven performance evaluations of military projects • Ministry of Finance Military Accounting System; evaluation using indicators, such as asset-liability ratios
Russia	• MoD • Federal Agency for State Property Management • Accounts Chamber

Abbreviations

CAPE	Cost Assessment and Program Evaluation
CCP	Chinese Communist Party
CMC	Central Military Commission
COCOM	combatant command
DoD	U.S. Department of Defense
DoDD	Department of Defense Directive
FYDP	Future Years Defense Program
GDP	gross domestic product
GLD	General Logistics Department
ICBM	intercontinental ballistic missile
IMF	International Monetary Fund
MiG	Mikoyan and Gurevich
MoD	Ministry of Defense (Russia)
MOF	Ministry of Finance (China)
NDS	National Defense Strategy
NPC	National People's Congress
O&M	operation and maintenance
OECD	Organisation for Economic Co-operation and Development
OMB	Office of Management and Budget
OSD	Office of the Secretary of Defense
PLA	People's Liberation Army
PPBE	Planning, Programming, Budgeting, and Execution
PPP	purchasing power parity
PRC	People's Republic of China
RDT&E	research, development, test, and evaluation
SAP	State Armaments Program
SDO	State Defense Order
SIPRI	Stockholm International Peace Research Institute
SOE	state-owned enterprise
VPK	Military-Industrial Commission [Voeynno Promyshlennaya Komissiya]

References

"20 Trillion Rubles Down the Drain. Largest State Arms Production Program in Russian History Halted Due to Failures in Ukraine" ["20 триллионов на ветер. Крупнейшая в российской истории госпрограмма производства оружия остановлена из-за провалов в Украине"], *Moscow Times*, November 11, 2022.

Ageev, Valery, "MiG-41: Real Breakthrough or Speculation" ["Миг-41: Реальный Прорыв Или Спекуляция"], *Nezavisimoe Voennoe Obozrenie*, September 17, 2020.

Anderson, Guy, "Russia Introduces Legislation to Crack Down on Defence Corruption," *Janes Defence Industry*, October 13, 2016.

Asanova, Antonina, "Pay for My Iskanders, How Russia Spends Windfall Profits from Oil and Gas on the War, a Study by *Novaya Gazeta Europe*" ["Оплатите мои «Искандеры» Как Россия тратит на войну сверхдоходы, полученные от торговли нефтью и газом: исследование «Новой газеты. Европа»"], *Novaya Gazeta Europe*, July 11, 2022.

Ashby, Mark, Caolionn O'Connell, Edward Geist, Jair Aguirre, Christian Curriden, and Jonathan Fujiwara, *Defense Acquisition in Russia and China*, RAND Corporation, RR-A113-1, 2021. As of February 28, 2023:
https://www.rand.org/pubs/research_reports/RRA113-1.html

Balut, Stephen S., Dennis C. Blair, Chester Arnold, John T. Hanley, Katy O. Hassig, Stanley A. Horowitz, David E. Hunter, Gong Xianfu, Jiang Shilang, Chen Yongxing, et al., *Proceedings of the Second IDA-CIISS Workshop: Common Security Challenges and Defense Personnel Costs*, Institute for Defense Analyses, January 2008.

Beliakova, Polina, "Russian Military's Corruption Quagmire," *Politico*, March 8, 2022.

Bernstein, Paul, and Dain Hancock, "China's Hypersonic Weapons," *Georgetown Journal of International Affairs*, January 27, 2021.

Blasko, Dennis J., Chas W. Freeman, Jr., Stanley A. Horowitz, Evan S. Medeiros, and James C. Mulvenon, *Defense-Related Spending in China: A Preliminary Analysis and Comparison with American Equivalents*, United States–China Policy Foundation, 2006.

Bodner, Matthew, "Russia's Once-Mighty Fighter Jet Firm MiG Struggling as Rivals Make Gains," *Moscow Times*, July 2, 2015.

Bogdanov, Konstantin, "Signed for 10 Years, Here Is What the New Government Arms Program Is Dedicated to for the Years 2018–2027" ["Подписались на 10 лет Чему посвящена новая госпрограмма вооружений, утвержденная на 2018–2027 годы"], *Izvestiya*, February 28, 2018.

Bowen, Andrew S., *Russian Arms Sales and Defense Industry*, Congressional Research Service, R46937, October 14, 2021.

Brimelow, Benjamin, "China Is Trying to Fix the Engine Problem Plaguing Its Fighter Jets," *Business Insider*, June 6, 2021.

Brodie, Bernard, *Strategy in the Missile Age*, RAND Corporation, CB-137-1, 1959. As of April 21, 2023:
https://www.rand.org/pubs/commercial_books/CB137-1.html

Budget Code of the Russian Federation, No. 145-FZ, July 31, 1998, effective January 1, 2023.

"Budget Law of the People's Republic of China," Xinhua, August 31, 2014.

"Budget of PLA Headquarters Focuses on Combat Power, Reducing Consumable Expenditures by 23%" ["解放军总部预算向战斗力聚焦 消耗性开支压减23%"], *China News*, June 18, 2013.

Budget.gov.ru, "The Budget Process" ["Бюджетный Процесс"], webpage, undated-a.

Budget.gov.ru, "Participants in the Budget Process" ["Участники бюджетного процесса"], webpage, undated-b.

Budget.gov.ru, "The Procedure and Terms for Compiling, Submitting, External Verification, Review and Approval of Budget Reporting, Unified Portal of the Budget System of the Russian Federation" ["Порядок и сроки составления, представления, внешней проверки, рассмотрения и утверждениябюджетной отчетности, Единый портал бюджетной системы российской федерации"], webpage, undated-c.

Burenok, V. M., ed., *Concept of Justification of Prospective Share of Power Components of the Military Organization of the Russian Federation*, Russian Academy of Missile and Artillery Sciences, 2018.

Burns, Robert, "Pentagon Rattled by Chinese Military Push on Multiple Fronts," Associated Press, November 1, 2021.

Center for Strategic and International Studies, "Missiles of Russia," webpage, August 10, 2021. As of February 16, 2023:
https://missilethreat.csis.org/country/russia

"The Central Military Commission Approves the Implementation of Military Expenditure Performance Management" ["中央军委批准推行军费绩效管理"], *Beijing News*, October 27, 2014.

Cheung, Tai Ming, *Innovate to Dominate: The Rise of the Chinese Techno-Security State*, Cornell University Press, 2022.

"Chinese Army to Tighten Expenditure," Xinhua, February 24, 2013.

Congressional Research Service, *A Defense Budget Primer*, RL30002, December 9, 1998.

Connolly, Richard, and Mathieu Boulégue, *Russia's New State Armament Programme: Implications for the Russian Armed Forces and Military Capabilities to 2027*, Chatham House, May 2018.

Cooper, Helene, Eric Schmitt, and Thomas Gibbons-Neff, "Soaring Death Toll Gives Grim Insight into Russian Tactics," *New York Times*, February 2, 2023.

Cooper, Julian, "Transforming Russia's Defense Industrial Base," *Survival*, Vol. 35, No. 4, Winter 1993.

Cooper, Julian, *Russian Military Expenditure: Data, Analysis and Issues*, Swedish Defense Research Agency, September 2013.

Cooper, Julian, "The Russian Budgetary Process and Defence: Finding the 'Golden Mean,'" *Post-Communist Economies*, Vol. 29, No. 4, 2017.

Cranny-Evans, Sam, and Olga Ivshina, "Corruption in the Russian Armed Forces," Royal United Services Institute, May 12, 2022.

Defense Intelligence Agency, *China Military Power: Modernizing a Force to Fight and Win*, 2019.

Demirjian, Karoun, Karen DeYoung, and Ellen Nakashima, "North Korea Covertly Supplying Russia with Artillery Rounds, U.S. Says," *Washington Post*, November 2, 2022.

Department of Defense Directive 7045.14, *The Planning, Programming, Budgeting, and Execution (PPBE) Process*, U.S. Department of Defense, August 29, 2017.

Ding Zhaozhong and Li Zhaochun, "Research on PPBE Defense Budget System Reform with Chinese Characteristics" ["中国特色PPBE 国防预算制度改革研究"], *Contemporary Economics* [当代经济], June 2016.

Dmitri [@wartranslated], "Continuation of the story with mobilized soldiers from the Moscow region aggressively talking to the officer about their lack of proper equipment and treatment," post on the X platform, November 13, 2022. As of February 17, 2023: https://twitter.com/wartranslated/status/1591829858598146050

Dmitriev, Denis, "The Government Has Classified a Quarter of All Russian Spending for 2023 (This Is a Record). We Do Not Know What Six and a Half Trillion Rubles Will Be Spent on—But It Is Probably the War and Annexations" ["Правительство засекретило четверть всех расходов России на 2023 год (это рекорд) Мы не знаем, на что потратят шесть с половиной триллионов рублей—но, вероятно, это война и аннексия"], Meduza Project, October 12, 2022.

DoD—*See* U.S. Department of Defense.

DoDD—*See* Department of Defense Directive.

"Employees of Uralvagonzavod Work Overtime Due to the State Defense Order" ["Сотрудников Уралвагонзавода переведут на сверхурочную работу из-за гособоронзаказа"], *Kommersant*, August 31, 2022.

Enthoven, Alain C., and K. Wayne Smith, *How Much Is Enough? Shaping the Defense Program, 1961–1969*, RAND Corporation, CB-403, 1971. As of April 21, 2023: https://www.rand.org/pubs/commercial_books/CB403.html

"Factbox: Where Have Russians Been Fleeing to Since Mobilisation Began?" Reuters, October 6, 2022.

Fang Zhengqi, "Overall Planning Measures for Resources for Building Our Military Under New Conditions" ["新形势下我军建设资源统筹对策"], *Military Economic Research* [军事经济研究], November 2015.

Federal Law of the Russian Federation No. 270-FZ, On the State Corporation for the Promotion of the Development, Manufacture, and Export of High-Tech Products ("Rostec"), November 23, 2007.

"Full Text of Xi Jinping's Report at the 19th CPC Congress," Xinhua, November 3, 2017.

Gaidar Institute for Economic Policy, "Sergei Tsukhlo Assesses the Labor Deficit in Industry" ["Сергей Цухло Оценил Дефицит Кадров в Промышленности"], November 11, 2022.

Gao Kai, "Strengthening Institutional Design to Improve Military Budget Execution" ["加强制度建设 确保军队预算执行力"], *Military Economic Research* [军事经济研究], February 2011.

Garamone, Jim, "Official Talks DoD Policy Role in Chinese Pacing Threat, Integrated Deterrence Role," U.S. Department of Defense, June 2, 2021.

Garnaut, John, "Rotting from Within: Investigating the Massive Corruption of the Chinese Military," *Foreign Policy*, April 16, 2012.

Geist, Edward, and Dara Massicot, "Understanding Putin's Nuclear 'Superweapons,'" *SAIS Review of International Affairs*, Vol. 39, No. 2, Summer–Fall 2019.

General M [@GenerMo], "@PhillipsPOBrien @JominiW @noclador @GlasnostGone @DefMon3 perhaps you will be interested, this barrel from the Russian BMP was filmed by Ukrainians," post on the X platform, July 24, 2022. As of January 5, 2023:
https://twitter.com/GenerMo/status/1551123902360961024

Global Defense Corp., "Undignified Death of T-14 Armata Main Battle Tank," February 21, 2020.

Golts, Aleksandr, "Russia's Rubezh Ballistic Missile Disappears off the Radar," *Eurasia Daily Monitor*, Vol. 14, No. 119, September 27, 2017.

Gouhua Hang, "China Moves Ahead on Accrual Accounting," *IMF Public Financial Management Blog*, December 4, 2015. As of February 28, 2023:
https://blog-pfm.imf.org/pfmblog/2015/12/china-moves-ahead-on-accrual-accounting-posted-by-gouhua-hang1-with-over-15000-budget-entities-in-central-government-an.html

Greenwalt, William, and Dan Patt, *Competing in Time: Ensuring Capability Advantage and Mission Success Through Adaptable Resource Allocation*, Hudson Institute, February 2021.

Han Guoxian [侯永波], "What Does Reform Bring National Defense Building?" ["改革给国防建设带来什么?"], *PLA Daily* [解放军报], January 25, 2016.

Heath, Timothy R., *China's New Governing Party Paradigm: Political Renewal and the Pursuit of National Rejuvenation*, Routledge, 2014.

Heginbotham, Eric, Michael Nixon, Forrest E. Morgan, Jacob L. Heim, Jeff Hagen, Sheng Tao Li, Jeffrey Engstrom, Martin C. Libicki, Paul DeLuca, David A. Shlapak, David R. Frelinger, Burgess Laird, Kyle Brady, and Lyle J. Morris, *The U.S.-China Military Scorecard: Forces, Geography, and the Evolving Balance of Power, 1996–2017*, RAND Corporation, RR-392-AF, 2015. As of February 28, 2023:
https://www.rand.org/pubs/research_reports/RR392.html

Heilmann, Sebastian, and Oliver Melton, "The Reinvention of Development Planning in China, 1993–2012," *Modern China*, Vol. 39, No. 6, November 2013.

Hitch, Charles J., and Roland N. McKean, *The Economics of Defense in the Nuclear Age*, RAND Corporation, R-346, 1960. As of April 21, 2023:
https://www.rand.org/pubs/reports/R346.html

Huai Fuli et al., "An Analysis of the Feasibility of Using PPBES as a Reference for Our Country's National Defense Budget System Reform" ["我国国防预算制度改革借鉴PPBES的可行性分析"], *Military Economics Research* [军事经济研究], July 2015.

Huang Ruixin [黄瑞新], "On PLA Carrying Out the Performance Budget System" ["对我军实行绩效预算制度的思考"], *Military Economics Research* [军事经济研究], June 2011.

Janes, "State Corporation Rostec," *Janes World Defence Industry*, September 7, 2022a.

Janes, "Defence Industry Country Overview: Russian Federation," *Janes World Defence Industry*, November 17, 2022b.

Ji, Elliot, "Great Leap Nowhere: The Challenges of China's Semiconductor Industry," *War on the Rocks*, February 23, 2023.

Jia Shiyu, "The Central Military Commission Approves the Implementation of Military Performance Management" ["中央军委批准推行军费绩效管理"], *People's Daily*, October 27, 2014.

Jurzyk, Emilia M., and Cian Ruane, "Resource Misallocation Among Listed Firms in China: The Evolving Role of State-Owned Enterprises," International Monetary Fund Working Paper No. 2021/075, March 12, 2021.

"'Kalashnikov' Was Appointed to Lead the Supply of Equipment, the Source Said," RIA Novosti, November 13, 2022.

Kraan, Dirk-Jan, Daniel Bergvall, Ian Hawkesworth, Valentina Kostyleva, and Matthias Witt, "Budgeting in Russia," *OECD Journal on Budgeting*, Vol. 8, No. 2, 2008.

LaGrone, Sam, "Russia Navy Faces Surface Modernization Delays Without Ukrainian Engines, Officials Pledge to Sue," USNI News, June 10, 2015.

Lam, Willy Wo-Lap, "Budget Surprise for China's Army," CNN, March 6, 2003.

Lawrence, Susan V., and Mari Y. Lee, *China's Political System in Charts: A Snapshot Before the 20th Party Congress*, Congressional Research Service, R46977, November 24, 2021.

Lee, Rob [@RALee85], "Photos comparing Ukrainian (below) and inferior Russian (above) first aid kits posted by Russian sources," post on the X platform, April 29, 2022. As of February 17, 2023:
https://twitter.com/RALee85/status/1519946804925767680

Li Zaiqian and Sun Zuo, "The Legal Regulation of China's National Defense Fund Allocation" ["论我国国防经费划拨的法律规制基于程序正当性的思考"], *Journal of PLA Nanjing Institute of Politics* [南京政治学学报], No. 3, 2013.

Luce, LeighAnn, and Erin Richter, "Handling Logistics in a Reformed PLA: The Long March Toward Joint Logistics," in Philip C. Saunders, Arthur S. Ding, Andrew Scobell, Andrew N. D. Yang, and Joel Wuthnow, eds., *Chairman Xi Remakes the PLA: Assessing Chinese Military Reforms*, National Defense University Press, 2019, pp. 257–292.

Luo Jiancheng and Geng Kui, "Improve the Strategic Evaluation System and Improve the Quality and Efficiency of Military Building" ["完善战略评估体系提升军队建设质量效益"], *China Military Science* [中国军事科学], August 20, 2021.

Luzin, Pavel, "The Kremlin's Economic Mobilization," *Eurasia Daily Monitor*, Vol. 19, No. 161, October 31, 2022.

Mazarr, Michael J., *The Societal Foundations of National Competitiveness*, RAND Corporation, RR-A499-1, 2022. As of April 21, 2023:
https://www.rand.org/pubs/research_reports/RRA499-1.html

McGarry, Brendan W., *Defense Primer: Planning, Programming, Budgeting and Execution (PPBE) Process*, Congressional Research Service, IF10429, January 27, 2020.

McGarry, Brendan W., *DOD Planning, Programming, Budgeting, and Execution: Overview and Selected Issues for Congress*, Congressional Research Service, R47178, July 11, 2022.

McGerty, Fenella, and Meia Nouwens, "China's Military Modernization Spurs Growth for State-Owned Enterprises," *Defense News*, August 8, 2022.

McKernan, Megan, Stephanie Young, Ryan Consaul, Michael Simpson, Sarah W. Denton, Anthony Vassalo, William Shelton, Devon Hill, Raphael S. Cohen, John P. Godges, Heidi Peters, and Lauren Skrabala, *Planning, Programming, Budgeting, and Execution in Comparative Organizations: Vol. 3, Case Studies of Selected Non-DoD Federal Agencies*, RAND Corporation, RR-A2195-3, 2024. As of January 12, 2024:
www.rand.org/pubs/research_reports/RRA2195-3

McKernan, Megan, Stephanie Young, Andrew Dowse, James Black, Devon Hill, Benjamin J. Sacks, Austin Wyatt, Nicolas Jouan, Yuliya Shokh, Jade Yeung, Raphael S. Cohen, John P. Godges, Heidi Peters, and Lauren Skrabala, *Planning, Programming, Budgeting, and Execution in Comparative Organizations: Vol. 2, Case Studies of Selected Allied and Partner Nations*, RAND Corporation, RR-A2195-2, 2024. As of January 12, 2024: www.rand.org/pubs/research_reports/RRA2195-2

McKernan, Megan, Stephanie Young, Timothy R. Heath, Dara Massicot, Andrew Dowse, Devon Hill, James Black, Ryan Consaul, Michael Simpson, Sarah W. Denton, Anthony Vassalo, Ivana Ke, Mark Stalczynski, Benjamin J. Sacks, Austin Wyatt, Jade Yeung, Nicolas Jouan, Yuliya Shokh, William Shelton, Raphael S. Cohen, John P. Godges, Heidi Peters, and Lauren Skrabala, *Planning, Programming, Budgeting, and Execution in Comparative Organizations: Vol. 4, Executive Summary*, RAND Corporation, RR-A2195-4, 2024. As of January 12, 2024: www.rand.org/pubs/research_reports/RRA2195-4

Meduza Project, "Russian Officials Are Constantly Talking About the Transition to a 'Mobilization Economy'—as in the Years of the Great Patriotic War. Is That Really Happening?" ["Российские чиновники постоянно говорят о переходе к «мобилизационной экономике»—как в годы Великой Отечественной войны. Это правда происходит?"], November 21, 2022a.

Meduza Project, "250 Convicts Will Serve Forced-Labor Sentences at Nizhny Tagil Tank and Armored-Vehicle Construction Plant," November 29, 2022b.

Meduza Project, "Russia Will Increase Funding for State Defense Orders by One and a Half Times" ["Россия увеличит финансирование гособоронзаказа в полтора раза"], November 30, 2022c.

Melton, Oliver, "China's Five-Year Planning System: Implications for the Reform Agenda," testimony before the U.S.-China Economic and Security Review Commission, April 22, 2015.

"Military Budgeting Reform Implementation Plan," Xinhua, March 22, 2001.

"The Military Prosecutor Called Theft in the Ministry of Defense 'Cosmic,'" ["Военный прокурор назвал воровство в Минобороны «космическим»"], Lenta.ru, January 11, 2012.

Mitzer, Stijn, and Jakub Janovsky, "Attack on Europe: Documenting Russian Equipment Losses During the 2022 Russian Invasion of Ukraine," Oryx, February 24, 2022.

Nan Tian and Fei Su, *A New Estimate of China's Military Expenditure*, Stockholm International Peace Research Institute, January 2021.

"NATO's Military Spending Exceeds Russian Army Budget by 20 Times, Says Security Chief," Tass, June 24, 2021.

Nikolski, Aleksei, Dmitry Grinkevich, and Irinia Sidorkova, "The Authorities Have Revised the Principles of Procurement for the Needs of the Armed Forces" ["Власти пересмотрели принципы закупок для нужд вооруженных сил"], *Vedomosti*, November 11, 2022.

"Northern Design Bureau Suspended Work on a Prototype Nuclear Destroyer" ["Северное ПКБ приостановило работу над перспективным атомным эсминцем"], Interfax, April 18, 2020.

Nouwens, Meia, and Lucie Béraud-Sudreau, *Assessing Chinese Defence Spending: Proposals for New Methodologies*, Institute for International Strategic Studies, March 31, 2020.

Odling-Smee, John, "The IMF and Russia in the 1990s," International Monetary Fund Working Paper No. 04/155, August 2004.

Pollpeter, Kevin, and Kenneth W. Allen, eds., *The PLA as Organization v.2.0*, China Aerospace Studies Institute, July 27, 2018.

Popper, Steven W., Marjory S. Blumenthal, Eugeniu Han, Sale Lilly, Lyle J. Morris, Caroline S. Wagner, Christopher A. Eusebi, Brian G. Carlson, and Alice Shih, *China's Propensity for Innovation in the 21st Century: Identifying Indicators of Future Outcomes*, RAND Corporation, RR-A208-1, 2020. As of February 28, 2023:
https://www.rand.org/pubs/research_reports/RRA208-1.html

Public Law 117–81, National Defense Authorization Act for Fiscal Year 2022, December 27, 2021.

Quinn, Alison, "Russia's Defence Minister 'Secretly Builds £12 Million Palace,' Say Campaigners," *The Telegraph*, October 29, 2015.

Radin, Andrew, Lynn E. Davis, Edward Geist, Eugeniu Han, Dara Massicot, Matthew Povlock, Clint Reach, Scott Boston, Samuel Charap, William Mackenzie, Katya Migacheva, Trevor Johnston, and Austin Long, *The Future of the Russian Military: Russia's Ground Combat Capabilities and Implications for U.S.-Russia Competition*, RAND Corporation, RR-3099-A, 2019. As of February 17, 2023:
https://www.rand.org/pubs/research_reports/RR3099.html

Robertson, Peter E., "The Real Military Balance: International Comparisons of Defense Spending," *Review of Income and Wealth*, Vol. 68, No. 3, September 2022.

Roggeveen, Sam, "China's New Aircraft Carrier Is Already Obsolete: But It's Still a Powerful Signal of Beijing's Ambitions in a Post-U.S. Asia," *Foreign Policy*, April 25, 2018.

Rozin, Igor, "Why Has Russia Merged Sukhoi and MiG Corporations into One?" *Russia Beyond*, April 8, 2021.

"Russia Bans Public Discussion of Army Strategy, Troop Morale, and Mobilization," *Moscow Times*, December 1, 2022.

"Russia Sends Mobilized Men to Ukraine Front After Days of Training—Activists," *Moscow Times*, September 27, 2022.

Russian Ministry of Finance, *Budget for Citizens to the Federal Law on the Federal Budget for 2020 and for the Planning Period of 2021 and 2022* [Бюджет Для Граждан к Федеральному закону о федеральном бюджете на 2020 год и на плановый период 2021 и 2022 годов], 2019.

Russian Treasury, *Reports on the Implementation of the Federal Budget* [Отчеты об исполнении федерального бюджета], 2012–2021.

"Russia's Labor-Starved Economy Pays Price of Putin's Call-Up," Bloomberg News, December 1, 2022.

Samus, Mykhailo, "Russia Postpones Future Aircraft Carrier Program," *Eurasia Daily Monitor*, Vol. 15, No. 69, May 7, 2018.

Saunders, Philip C., Arthur S. Ding, Andrew Scobell, Andrew N. D. Yang, and Joel Wuthnow, eds., *Chairman Xi Remakes the PLA: Assessing Chinese Military Reforms*, National Defense University Press, 2019.

Schneider, Mark, "Lessons from Russian Missile Performance in Ukraine," *Proceedings*, Vol. 148/10/1436, October 2022.

Scobell, Andrew, *Chinese Army Building in the Era of Jiang Zemin*, Strategic Studies Institute, U.S. Army War College, July 2000.

Section 809 Panel, *Report of the Advisory Panel on Streamlining and Codifying Acquisition Regulations*, Vol. 2 of 3, June 2018.

Seldin, Jeff, "US Defense Officials: China Is Leading in Hypersonic Weapons," *Voice of America*, March 10, 2023.

Sevastopulo, Demetri, and Kathrin Hille, "China Tests New Space Capability with Hypersonic Missile," *Financial Times*, October 16, 2021.

Sherwood, Monika, *Medium-Term Budgetary Frameworks in the EU Member States*, European Commission, European Economy Discussion Paper 021, December 2015.

Shinkman, Paul D., "How Russian Corruption Is Foiling Putin's Army in Ukraine," *U.S. News and World Report*, August 31, 2022.

SIPRI—*See* Stockholm International Peace Research Institute.

Speciale, Stephen, and Wayne B. Sullivan II, "DoD Financial Management—More Money, More Problems," Defense Acquisition University, September 1, 2019.

Staalesen, Atle, "Putin Takes a Look at New Aircraft Carrier," *Barents Observer*, January 10, 2020.

Starchak, Maxim, "Russia Terminates Development of New Rail-Mobile Ballistic Missile," *Eurasia Daily Monitor*, Vol. 14, No. 162, December 13, 2017.

Starchak, Maxim, "Missed Targets: The Struggles of Russia's Missile Industry," Center for European Policy Analysis, June 27, 2022.

State Council Information Office of the People's Republic of China, *China's National Defense*, December 11, 2006.

State Council Information Office of the People's Republic of China, *China's Military Strategy*, May 27, 2015.

State Council Information Office of the People's Republic of China, *China's National Defense in the New Era*, June 24, 2019.

State Duma of the Federal Assembly of the Russian Federation, "How Is the Federal Budget Approved?" ["Как принимается федеральный бюджет"], September 30, 2021.

Stockholm International Peace Research Institute, "SIPRI Military Expenditure Database," homepage, undated. As of March 17, 2023:
https://milex.sipri.org/sipri

Stockholm International Peace Research Institute, "Top List Trend-Indicator Value (TIV) of Arms Imports or Exports for a Selection of the Largest Suppliers or Recipients, Along with the TIV of Global Arms Imports or Exports," dataset, October 31, 2022. As of March 17, 2023:
https://armstrade.sipri.org/armstrade/page/toplist.php

Sun Xingwei, Qui Mingjie, and Li Jian, "The Relevant Person in Charge of the CMC Logistic Support Department Finance Bureau Answered Reporters' Questions on the Latest Expense Settlement and Reimbursement Regulations," ["军委后勤保障部财务局有关负责人就最新经费结算报销规定问题答记者问"], *PLA Daily*, May 20, 2019.

Tao Shengxu Jinzhang, "PLA to Comprehensively Promote the Standardization of Business Funds" ["全军全面推进事业经费标准化建设"], *PLA Daily*, October 22, 2014.

Tegler, Eric, "A New Kremlin 'Committee' Won't Accelerate Production of Weapons for Russian Troops in Ukraine," *Forbes*, October 26, 2022.

Transparency International Defence and Security, "Russia," Government Defence Integrity Index 2020, June 2019–May 2020.

United Nations Office for Disarmament Affairs, "Military Expenditures Database," webpage, undated. As of February 28, 2023:
https://milex.un-arm.org

U.S. Code, Title 10, Armed Forces, Section 3131, Availability of Appropriations.

U.S. Department of Defense, *2022 National Defense Strategy of the United States of America*, 2022.

Vorobyev, Aleksander, "Defense Companies Are Unable to Service Loans" ["оборонные предприятия не справлются с обслуживанием кредитов"], *Vedomosti*, October 17, 2019.

Wang Zhe, Zhang Xing, Qi Zhihong, and Wang Qingjuan, "Analysis on the Construction of the National Defense Medium-Term Budget Management System" ["国防预算中期管理制度的构建分析"], *Review of Economic Research* [经济研究参考], 2017.

Weinbaum, Cortney, Caolionn O'Connell, Steven W. Popper, M. Scott Bond, Hannah Jane Byrne, Christian Curriden, Gregory Weider Fauerbach, Sale Lilly, Jared Mondschein, and Jon Schmid, *Assessing Systemic Strengths and Vulnerabilities of China's Defense Industrial Base: With a Repeatable Methodology for Other Countries*, RAND Corporation, RR-A930-1, 2022. As of February 28, 2023:
https://www.rand.org/pubs/research_reports/RRA930-1.html

Wezeman, Siemon T., "Russia's Military Spending: Frequently Asked Questions," Stockholm International Peace Research Institute, April 27, 2020.

"'Where Did They Disappear To?' Russian MP Says 1.5 Million Military Uniforms Are Missing," *Novaya Gazeta Europe*, October 2, 2022.

Wingender, Philippe, "Intergovernmental Fiscal Reform in China," International Monetary Fund Working Paper No. 18/88, April 13, 2018.

Wong, Christine, "Plus ça Change: Three Decades of Fiscal Policy and Central-Local Relations in China," *China: An International Journal*, Vol. 19, No. 4, November 2021.

Wood, Peter, Alden Wahlstrom, and Roger Cliff, *China's Aeroengine Industry*, China Aerospace Studies Institute, March 2020.

Wuthnow, Joel, and M. Taylor Fravel, "China's Military Strategy for a 'New Era': Some Change, More Continuity, and Tantalizing Hints," *Journal of Strategic Studies*, March 8, 2022.

"Xi Focus: PLA Striving to Build World Class Military Under Xi's Leadership," Xinhua, August 2, 2022.

"Xi Jinping Signs an Order: The PLA Audit Office Is Placed Under the Central Military Commission" ["习近平签署命令:解放军审计署划归中央军委建制"], Xinhua, November 6, 2014.

Xin Zhiming, "Revised Budget Law to Have Far Reaching Effect," *China Daily*, September 11, 2014.

Xu Mingzhi, "Diagnosis and Treatment of Weakened Enforcement on Military Budget" ["军队预算执行力弱化诊疗"], *Military Economic Research* [军事经济研究], November 2010.

Yang Shipeng and Zeng Lingbo, "Commentary on the Focus of Military Accounting System Reforms" ["军队会计制度改革焦点评述"], *Military Economic Research* [军事经济研究], July 2006.

Zhang Yang, Sun Min, and Li Wenzhong, "Government Budget Performance Management and Implications for Military Budget Management" ["政府预算绩效管理及对军队预算管理的启示"], *China Management Informationization*, Vol. 24, No. 18, September 2021.

89

Zhang Yunbi, "Reform Advisors Come into View," *China Daily*, August 2, 2016.

Zhao Lei, "China to Raise Military Budget by 7.1% This Year," *China Daily*, March 6, 2022.